"Many have been blessed through the years by what David has said. For years, our church was blessed by what David did, and the fruit is still growing. He doesn't just teach the wisdom in this book; he puts it into practice. This man walks his talk. Read and apply!"

—**Rick Atchley,** Senior Teaching Minister, The Hills Church

"I hope every youth leader pays attention to David's wise insights. *Practical Wisdom for Youth Ministry* helps rookies start ministry on the right trajectory and helps veterans adjust their lives and ministries to experience all God has for them."

—**Kara Powell,** PhD, Executive Director of the Fuller Youth Institute and coauthor of *Growing Young* and *Sticky Faith*

"*Practical Wisdom for Youth Ministry* lies at the crucial intersection in youth ministry today: the corner of academics, theology, and praxis. Fraze combines these elements, undergirding this practical text with a foundation of theology and academics. It is an invaluable read for those concerned with youth ministry—future youth ministers, volunteers, parent chaperones, and church leaders. Drawing from over thirty years of experience in youth ministry, Fraze effectively places the focus on both the nuts and bolts of youth ministry and the philosophical and theological principles behind those nuts and bolts."

—**Walter Surdacki,** DMin, Associate Professor of Bible & Ministry, Lipscomb University

"For over three decades, I've been equipping college students to pursue their passion in youth ministry, and this book says so many wonderful, important, mission-critical things that I want them to hear! I love the tone, the content, the depth, and the format of this book. Trust me, *any* youthworker—rookie, veteran, or volunteer— will find it a worthwhile read."

—**Duffy Robbins,** Professor of Youth Ministry, Eastern University

"Wisdom never goes out of date. It is always needed. My good friend and youth ministry co-laborer David Fraze has written a timely book that we certainly need as we strive for God-honoring excellence in youth ministry. For the new youthworker, this book will set you on a course to flourish in your work. And for those of us who have been doing this for quite some time, checkups are always necessary."

—**Dr. Walt Mueller,** President, Center for Parent/Youth Understanding

"This book is one of the most practical resources on student ministry I have ever read. It covers a wide range of issues, but it also provides detailed applications for immediate use in various contexts. David speaks from the trenches of ministry, and his passion comes through loud and clear. I highly recommend this book, especially for younger ministers who are just getting started."

—**Dave Blanchard,** Director of Student Ministry, West Houston Church of Christ

"David is a good friend, and he's written a terrific book with practical tips for reaching young people. While he might not call himself an expert, he is. You won't just find ideas for how to reach kids in these pages; you'll discover more about your own faith."

—**Bob Goff,** Chief Balloon Inflator and author of *Love Does*

"There are very few credentialed practitioners, both practical and academic, who could deliver such a book. In *Practical Wisdom for Youth Ministry*, David embodies the "blue-collar scholar" at his best, offering years of pragmatic knowledge distilled into a readable, grounded, and praxiologically rich presentation that will benefit youth ministers at all levels of experience."

—**Dr. Steven Bonner,** Affiliate Faculty for Lipscomb University, Director of the Vocati Institute, and President of the Association of Youth Ministry Educators

"People who work with adolescents truly love God and love others— Jesus' greatest commands. Having worked as a youth minister for twenty-five years and with other youth ministers for over thirty years, I welcome Fraze's contribution to the conversation of how we minister to young people. This book is very practical in a time when we need to put our faith into action with young people. The principles are solid, and the stories and experiences are valuable and replicable."

—**Dudley Chancey,** PhD, Professor of Ministry,
Oklahoma Christian University

"My friend gave his son a toolbox when he got married. It contained all the basic tools one might need—hammer, screwdriver, pliers. The son told me it was one of the best gifts he received. My friend David Fraze has done the same for new youth ministers with this book. He gives you the youth ministry basics you need in simple, practical, bite-sized chunks. Get this tool box. You'll love it!"

—**Jeff Walling,** Director, Youth Leadership Initiative,
Pepperdine University

"David brings his experiences to the pages of the book in your hands. If you implement the wisdom contained in this book, it will make you a better youth minister. It will help a confused parent become a more confident parent. It will encourage the incredible youth volunteers who understand the importance of reaching the next generation for Christ."

—**Robert Oglesby Jr.,** Director of the Center for Youth and Family
Ministry, Abilene Christian University

"*Practical Wisdom for Youth Ministry* is a perfect title for this book. The Bible is the foundation on which youth ministers teach, guide, and mentor, and the wisdom in these pages begins with God's Word. Featuring an in-the-trenches kind of practical experience, this book is full of mature, seasoned, and tested advice for the new or volunteer youth minister."

—**Johnny Markham,** Family Minister, College Hills Church of Christ

"I would recommend this book to all youth ministers—beginning or experienced. It is one of the most practical approaches to youth ministry I've ever seen. I have worked beside David in a ministry setting, and I've seen him put this teaching into practice. My son hopes to go into youth ministry someday. I'll make sure he has a copy of this book!"

—**Chris Hatchett,** Campus Minister, The Hills Church

"David is of the rare breed of youth ministers who can think locally and globally at the same time. In *Practical Wisdom for Youth Ministry*, David masterfully addresses the immediate needs of the local youthworker within the changing global landscape of youth ministry. If you're new to youth ministry, this book is essential. If you're a veteran youthworker, this book will help you to recalibrate in a new era of youth ministry."

—**Jacob Eckeberger,** Director of Resource Development,
Youth Specialties

"As a person who loves to see others develop for and in ministry, I see this book as a must-read for anyone serving in student ministry. Not only is it thorough in its philosophical approach to ministry, but it is also practical, and it serves as an invitation and inspiration to create our own stories in ministry."

—**Brian Aaby,** Director of Youth Specialties Search & Coaching

Practical Wisdom for Youth Ministry is the book every youth minister should read with their interns when the summer begins. It should be required reading for every college youth ministry course and a close companion to everyone engaged in student ministry. My friend David's book will impact the youth ministry world for decades.

—**Josh Ross,** Lead Minister, Sycamore View Church, and author
of *Re\entry*

Only a great communicator could pack three decades worth of insights into one resource. If David's experience as a leader in youth ministry is an iceberg, then *Practical Wisdom for Youth Ministry* is the tip. He'll draw you in with his stories and humor, but you'll keep reading because of his wisdom.

—**Scott Adair,** DMin, Associate Professor of Bible and Ministry,
Director of the Center for Family Ministries, Harding University

"David is one of the top youth minister educators and practitioners. His uplifting messages inspire youth and adults to take action!"

—**Jim Sundberg,** former MLB player and author

"I have never seen someone with so much passion for student ministry or with the unique ability to navigate teen culture as well as be a resource for parents and adults."

—**James Herman,** Lead Student Minister, The Hills Church

PRACTICAL WISDOM

FOR
YOUTH MINISTRY

PRACTICAL WISDOM

FOR
YOUTH MINISTRY

THE NOT-SO-SIMPLE TRUTHS THAT MATTER

DAVID FRAZE

LEAFWOOD
PUBLISHERS
an imprint of Abilene Christian University Press

PRACTICAL WISDOM FOR YOUTH MINISTRY
The Not-So-Simple Truths That Matter

LEAFWOOD
PUBLISHERS
an imprint of Abilene Christian University Press

LIBRARY OF CONGRESS CATALOGING-IN-PUBLICATION DATA
Names: Fraze, David, 1968- author.
Title: Practical wisdom for youth ministry : the not-so-simple truths that matter / David Fraze.
Description: Abilene : Leafwood Publishers, 2018. | Includes bibliographical references.
Identifiers: LCCN 2017044234 | ISBN 9780891124344 (pbk.)
Subjects: LCSH: Church work with youth.
Classification: LCC BV4447 .F667 2018 | DDC 259/.23—dc23
LC record available at https://lccn.loc.gov/ 2017044234

Cover design by ThinkPen Design
Interior text design by Sandy Armstrong, Strong Design

Leafwood Publishers is an imprint of Abilene Christian University Press
ACU Box 29138
Abilene, Texas 79699

1-877-816-4455
www.leafwoodpublishers.com

18 19 20 21 22 23 / 7 6 5 4 3 2 1

To Lisa:

I love you. You are my best friend.
I still can't believe we get to spend each day together.
As those who know us will attest, I out-punted my
coverage when I married you. Thank you for your
unwavering support and love.

To Braeden and Shelbee:

Being your dad is my greatest joy.
Thank you for your understanding and support
in the times you share your dad with other people.
I love you and am proud of you both.

CONTENTS

ACKNOWLEDGMENTS

I love how Maj. Dick Winters of the famed 101st Airborne, in the TV series *Band of Brothers*, responded when his grandson asked, "Grandpa, were you a hero in the war?"

"No, but I served in a company of heroes," responded Winters.[1]

I am honored and blessed to work in youth ministry alongside a company of heroes, many of whom have deeply influenced the writing of this book. There are dozens of ministry heroes with whom I have served for years in the trenches of youth work. In fear of leaving someone out, I will not list all those who have and continue to serve. I stand on the shoulders of great men and women. I hope you find your voice in the pages of this book.

Professors from Lubbock Christian University, Abilene Christian University, Texas Tech University, Lipscomb University, and Fuller Theological Seminary stand as intellectual and inspirational heroes.

Professional heroes Jason Herman, Duffy Robbins, Walt Mueller, Kara Powell, Brad Griffin, Brian Aaby, Jacob Eckeberger, Guy Brown, Josh Ross, and Dudley Chancey all personally encouraged me to write and add my voice to youth ministry. Thank you for the challenge and support. Chap Clark, thank you for challenging me to think deeply about youth ministry, providing opportunities, and loving my family. I finally wrote that book.

Scott Jarvis, Steven Esquivel, Philip Nichols, Brad Teague, Terri Groves, Jason Ratliff, and John Duncan, my original band of youth ministry heroes, thank you for a lifetime of memories. You push me and hold me accountable to being the best man, husband, dad, and youth minister I can be.

I have been honored to work with some incredible churches. Legacy Church of Christ, Highland Church of Christ, Green Lawn Church of Christ, South Plains Church of Christ, Broadway Church of Christ, and The Hills Church are filled with heroic followers of Christ who have left a deep impact on my life, an impact I hope you can see in these pages.

Thank you to the coaches, players, and staff of the Richland High School football team. Your support during the writing of this book was appreciated.

My parents, Henry and Lana Fraze, are my original heroes. Thank you for raising me in a loving, supportive, Christ-centered home. You put flesh on faith. Thank you to my older sisters Carol and Laura for providing much of the material for my stories.

Thank you, Leafwood Publishers, for your wonderful editorial work and partnership in the development of this book.

And thank you to my Rufe Snow Starbucks for the coffee and for being my office away from the office. Whether you knew it or not, you have helped impact eternity.

FOREWORD

by Chap Clark

I have known David for a long time.

I know his marriage. I know his children, and I have been around the students he has worked with. I have been in his church and with the adults he helps to train and lead into healthy and sacrificial ministry. I was his teacher when he got his doctorate, watched him interact with other youth ministry leaders, and even graded his papers. For several years we worked together to train parents and youthworkers.

My friend David is making a bold claim with his title *Practical Wisdom for Youth Ministry: The Not-So-Simple Truths That Matter*. Two words that especially catch my eye as I venture in are "Wisdom" and "Truths." Add to that the additional qualifier of the two colossal promises explicit in these two words "That Matter," and you've either got an absolute "must have" or a "don't get me near that thing."

This book fits the first category.

I am of the temperament where I really care about the things that actually matter, and I run hard and fast from those that do not seem to matter much at all. An argument, for example, that seems to be based more on feelings than facts doesn't get much attention from me. And impassioned pleas that are meant to evoke a response from me without anything to actually connect it to my reality is an immediate turn off. Scholars tell us the least productive form of communication is what's referred to as the "one-sided appeal," more popularly known as the debate. The reason? In a one-sided appeal, the sender is so convinced in his or her position or perspective that the sole job of the communicator (writer, speaker, pastor, youth pastor, etc.) in engaging other people is to persuade them to the communicator's side, without any acknowledgment that the hearer may have a different take. Research has shown that 80 percent of the time, all things being equal, the one-sided approach to passing on information causes another person to move *away* from the source rather than toward it. Typically, these kinds of appeals are the worst. Not only does what someone says not matter to the hearer, at the end of the day they push their hearers further away from themselves and their message.

Books can be like that. I read a lot of books. Some are okay, a very few are great, and most are a waste of time. Writing is, of course, by definition a one-sided appeal. An author, by necessity, must establish credibility and the stance that he or she is an expert, or they shouldn't be writing in the first place (it used to be the publisher's job to make sure this was the case, but with the plethora of options available to writers today, it is hard to tell who is an *actual* expert and who just has a strong opinion). So when a book comes around telling me that there is "wisdom" to be found in these pages, and to top it off there is a promise that "truths that matter" will be shared, you might wonder, "Seriously?"

Let me reassure you. *Practical Wisdom for Youth Ministry* is one of those rare, great books. David knows what he's talking about. He shares his years of experience, but even more than that, he brings authentic, honest, and solid theological reflection to this book. I have a pretty good handle on youth ministry: our history, our theology (such as it is), and our practice. The wisdom that David shares is not theoretical, it's practical. The truths he offers are not simple or easy—and he tells us that right in the title! I invite you to come alongside David as he wades through that wisdom and shares about the truths that really matter.

I am not only proud of David for this book, I'm grateful that David waited until this point of his life to write the right book, and this is it. This is a book that matters.

Chap Clark, PhD (Human Communication, University of Denver)
Professor of Youth, Family, and Culture, Fuller Theological Seminary, and author of *Hurt 2.0: Inside the World of Today's Teenagers*

INTRODUCTION

"I voted for the other guy!"

What?! My first full-time youth ministry job and that is what came out of the mouth of one of my "kids" at the door of the youth room. Wow! Needless to say, the encounter was a little discouraging. Can you relate?

You nailed the interview, received the offer, moved to your new location, unpacked your office, and now what? Anxiety and panic begin creeping into your thoughts.

What if they don't like my teaching?

What if a parent thinks I am too young (or old).

I am pretty sure the custodian already hates me.

I'm not sure, but I think I just heard a kid say "what a dork" as I walked by.

Don't panic, all youth ministers have muttered these desperate words to themselves at least once in their youth ministry career. And the kid who voted for the other guy? Trent is now a talented youth ministry veteran and close friend who has experienced his own share of bad introductions. And yes, he still reminds me that he voted for the other guy.

Welcome to youth ministry!

WHY I WROTE THIS BOOK

I wrote this book with the new youth minister in mind. I want to help get you through that "what do I do now?" moment. There will be moments when you need help and direction quickly. You will not have the time to look through your class notes, search the web, or read a lengthy book. This book is for you.

I wrote this book with the volunteer youthworker in mind. You are the true heroes of youth ministry, and you may be asked to serve in areas in which you feel you have little or no training. You need pointers and practical advice quickly. This book is for you.

I also wrote this book with the seminary or university student in mind. You are going to learn a lot about teenage culture, adolescence, family systems, theology, communication, and Scripture. Drink deeply and take this ministry seriously. We need you to be prepared and ready to share your unique giftedness with students. This book will provide a starting place for your study.

Practical Wisdom for Youth Ministry is not intended to be an exhaustive look into youth ministry practice. I acknowledge that more topics could have been added to the content. I am also certain that other youth ministry professionals are wondering why other topics did not make the cut. There are two reasons why some topics made the cut (or a brief mention) and others did not. First, some excluded topics, like counseling troubled students, demand a higher level of expertise to safely provide direction. Second, some topics were given a brief mention because they have been extensively written about and flood the youth ministry market. In the end, a choice had to be made.

HOW TO READ THIS BOOK

All new appliances, computers, televisions, phones, power tools, gaming systems, and assembly-required furniture come with a full set of instructions for setup and use. However, because we are impatient and ready to use our purchase quickly, most of these come with a one-page, easy-to-understand set of quick startup instructions.

I like the quick startup instructions. Depending on the complexity of the startup, most instruction guides are one to four pages max. The steps are easy to follow and filled with valuable information, and they typically let you know when you are out of your league and need to open up the complete set of instructions.

The book you are holding is a quick-start guide for youth ministry. Depending on the complexity of the topic, most chapters are concise. The steps are easy to follow and are sandwiched between actual youth ministry stories that highlight the need for and application of the truth being discussed. The information is arranged in three parts:

* **Why:** Theological underpinnings and support for the truth
* **How:** Practical application and discussion of the truth
* **Now:** First-steps suggestions for strengthening the truth or making the truth a part of your youth ministry context

Helpful endnotes are provided for clarification and deeper study.

In short, there is no "right way" to read this book. You can read front to back or skip around to the topic you need quick startup assistance with right now. If in doubt, start with Youth Ministry Matters and browse the End Matter material.

Wherever you start, thank you for allowing me to join you in your youth ministry journey. It is great to have you on the team.

THE BIBLE
MATTERS

"Gentlemen, if you ever let your mind wander to imagining what a girl looks like naked, you are sinning!"

The one who delivered these words had such conviction and passion as he spoke about Jesus's teaching on lustful looks and adultery. Honestly, I don't remember the name of the teacher—I just remember my shame. I was in junior high school and certainly headed for hell. Even though I tried, I just could not stop thinking about girls. And sometimes, like when the teacher said the word "naked," I started to wonder what a girl really looked like without clothes.

Yep, hell bound for sure. I am certain many more junior high kids in the audience felt the same shame and burden. Why? Because a scripture was irresponsibly and incorrectly taught to a group of hormonally charged middle school kids.

Before you start sending hate messages to my inbox, go back and study what Jesus was actually talking about when using the word "lust." Also, realize I am not claiming that "naked imagining" should be encouraged (that can lead one to lustful thoughts). Junior high kids do not need encouragement for their minds to wander and wonder. As is true for every desire, they must master their impulses.

My purpose here is not to unpack a difficult passage. I bring this story from my past to our present to demonstrate the damage that can occur when the Bible is used improperly. Remember the power you hold in your words as you teach students.

> For the word of God is alive and active. Sharper than any double-edged sword, it penetrates even to dividing soul and spirit, joints and marrow; it judges the thoughts and attitudes of the heart (Heb. 4:12).

TRUTH: THE BIBLE MATTERS.

WHY?

The Bible is the foundation on which youth ministers teach, preach, and mentor. It is my conviction that all other information (psychological, sociological, historical, and cultural) should be filtered through the lens of Scripture.

> All Scripture is God-breathed and is useful for teaching, rebuking, correcting and training in righteousness, so that the servant of God may be thoroughly equipped for every good work (2 Tim. 3:16–17).

Why the need for such an obvious statement? Two reasons. One, if not careful, youth ministers may be tempted to think the power of their teaching, preaching, and mentoring resides in their ability to turn an illustration, keep an audience's attention, and give sage advice. I certainly hope a youth minister is skilled in delivery, but the power is in the Word. Two, the idea that the Bible provides the foundation on which all other sources of truth are evaluated is being challenged.[1] The Bible is not just another book—it is the book for all ministry, including youth ministry.

There is something special happening when the Word of God is taught, preached, and shared with those in need of direction. God speaks. Truth is discovered. Lives are changed.

It takes work to study and use the Bible. Without making it a priority, the activity of a youth minister often leaves little time for Bible study, which results in messages and mentoring that are proof-texting[2] adventures at best. The following verse has always propelled my preparation in Scripture:

> Not many of you should become teachers, my fellow
> believers, because you know that we who teach will
> be judged more strictly (James 3:1).

We better be sure of what we have to share when we speak. Study.

HOW?

The Bible is a relevant and useful tool for youth ministry. If you don't believe that truth, pick up the Bible, dig deep, and challenge your assumption. You may discover or rediscover just how relevant and useful the Word of God is in ministry to teenagers. If you are reading this book, I assume that you have some type of regard for the Bible. With that assumption in mind, the following suggestions are for keeping the Bible alive in your life and that of your students.

Read the Bible. As youth ministers, it's easy to get into the habit of reading to teach instead of reading to learn. Yes, you need to read and study for teaching moments. But when do you read for your own personal growth? Based on my experience, don't rationalize and claim that reading for others is the same as reading for yourself. This does not work for long and leaves you feeling dry and uninspired, a bad place to be for a youth minister. If you need more reading for yourself, try this:

* Read a chapter in Psalms or Proverbs every day.
* Read the same section of Scripture every day for a week.
* Read a Gospel every week.
* Start a read-through-the-Bible plan.
* Pick a word and dive into your concordance.
* Memorize Scripture (you will be amazed how these truths come out in your mentoring).

Start reading for you! After reading, be slow to teach what you have learned. Let what you read resonate and make an impact inside of you before sharing with others.

Use the Bible—Part 1. It is so easy to find an awesome illustration (video, story, or song) and base an entire lesson around that piece. I have done this a number of times, and I am not saying it's a bad thing. But if that's what you always do to prepare your weekly messages, then that's not so good. Use the Bible.

One way to use the Bible for teaching is to actually use it in the planning of your teaching calendar:

* Pick a book, character, topic, or theological concept from the Bible.
* Study what you have chosen.
* Allow your lesson plans to form naturally from your study (it will happen; trust me on this).
* Build practical and relevant application of Scripture once the study is complete.

As mentioned, youth ministers can develop lesson plans topically from the real or perceived needs of their students. Certainly, such teaching has its place and makes use of Scripture. However, too much of this approach can leave students unable and intimidated to navigate the Bible on their own. Do not be afraid to teach a book, character, topic, or theological concept from the Bible. It is much more relevant to teenagers than you might think.

Use the Bible—Part 2. This may sound too simplistic, but use the Bible, and ask your students to use the Bible in your lessons and activities. Whatever the media (book, phone app, etc.), get your students into the Word. If you use presentation software, get those scriptures on the screen and encourage the audience to follow along.

If it appears difficult for youth ministers to use the Bible in their teachings, how much more difficult is it for their students to use the Bible in their own lives? Here are some tips to help your students get into the reading of the Bible:

* Share helpful apps that can get them on a reading plan and provide helpful commentary (I really like YouVersion).
* Give them scriptures to memorize after a lesson.
* Create quiet times at retreats and camps in which you have them read the Bible (or print a section on which you want them to concentrate).
* Issue group challenges in which a certain book or section of Scripture is to be read, and follow up on what they have read (don't be gimmicky, challenge their passion, and ask them to join you in the reading).

* Give your students (and adults) a clear understanding of how the Bible is arranged and suggestions on where to start reading (I recommend the Gospels and Psalms/Proverbs as a starting place—it's always good to start with Jesus).

Such steps help take the intimidation of Bible study away. Ultimately, if you want students to read the Bible, then the adults around them have to lead the way.

Don't commit the sin of making the Bible boring. This may not be a sin, but it should be! There is so much great material in the Bible. If you dig deep, you will find that even the most "boring" sections of Scripture are anything but boring. The Bible is filled with difficult sections. Don't give up! There are a number of great resources to help you in your journey.[3]

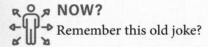

NOW?

Remember this old joke?

> Question: "How do you eat an elephant?"
> Answer: "One bite at a time."

You must commit to start somewhere. How about starting today? This book will wait.

Put this book down, pick up your Bible, and start reading. You can come back to this book tomorrow.

"I wanted to quit."

I had finished three semesters of Bible in college and had one internship under my belt. On the outside, everything was going well, but I was done. Why? I had studied and taught the

Bible for almost a full year and a half without much relief. I was saying the right things but was feeling very little. I was a burned-out Bible major who needed some fire. I was looking for anything to keep me going. So I decided to go back to the basics. I took my Bible and a journal, went to a local park, and read the Gospel of John with a desperate prayer on my lips to God: "Let me experience the joy I had when I first heard this story." God answered my prayer.

Almost thirty years later, the Father still meets me in those moments. He will meet you as well.

CONCLUDING TRUTH: THE BIBLE MATTERS.

BOUNDARIES
MATTER

"Hey, intern, you need to break up your harem and get back to work!"

This is what I shouted to my intern as he sat on a bench with at least four girls around him and one sitting on his lap. Perhaps I was a little dramatic, and he was clearly agitated, but what followed was a long discussion concerning appropriate boundaries in youth ministry. I am sure that if I had it to do over again, I would not have shouted the "harem" comment. But the scene brought back a number of inappropriate boundary-crossing stories, repeated or witnessed, that I did not want this young man to repeat.

One such boundary crossing happened in the first year of my youth ministry. Lisa and I had gone into the youth minister hangout room at a popular summer camp. It was awesome being on the "other side" for the first time as a full-time youth minister. This room was filled with several of my youth ministry heroes, one of whom was sitting at a table playing cards with a few other legends of youth ministry. Just as Lisa and I started to approach the table, a high-school-age young lady (not his daughter) jumped into the lap of this card-playing hero. He then proceeded to pat her on the thigh and call her "sweetheart." What!? I know.

Lisa and I did not know what to do or say, so we turned around and left the room feeling rather disturbed and disillusioned. Once outside, Lisa indicated she would not be pleased if I let a girl sit on my lap and repeat the actions we had witnessed in that room. I agreed she should be upset. And then we were confused. Why did he think that was appropriate? Was this not a boundary concern for this man? Why did his friends not say anything? From that point on, we decided to be friends who said something and to gather friends who would say something to each of us when needed.

TRUTH: BOUNDARIES MATTER.

WHY?

Youth ministers are natural boundary setters. We passionately communicate and plead with teenagers to not cross that line, to stay with the group, to avoid this area, be at the bus at 3:30 sharp, stop sharing blankets, stop pranking the adult volunteers. Boundaries are not intended to be a pharisaical burden on people. Boundaries are set up so difficulties can be minimized or avoided. For example, there are boundaries between the elephants and visitors at a zoo. Why? Without the boundaries, it would be chaotic and a bit of a safety issue. The Bible is filled with all types of boundary statements that are intended to help people avoid misunderstandings, difficulties, conflicts, and sinful behaviors.

> When the Most High gave the nations their
> inheritance, when he divided all mankind, he set up

boundaries for the peoples according to the number of the sons of Israel (Deut. 32:8).

Now then, my sons, listen to me; do not turn aside from what I say. Keep to a path far from her [adulteress], do not go near the door of her house (Prov. 5:7–8).

If your right eye causes you to stumble, gouge it out and throw it away. It is better for you to lose one part of your body than for your whole body to be thrown into hell. And if your right hand causes you to stumble, cut it off and throw it away. It is better for you to lose one part of your body than for your whole body to go into hell (Matt. 5:29–30).

But among you there must not be even a hint of sexual immorality, or of any kind of impurity, or of greed, because these are improper for God's holy people (Eph. 5:3).

Speed limits, nutritional information, entertainment ratings, and property laws are all examples of boundaries that have been given to help human beings better govern their personal and communal lives. We are free to ignore and break those boundaries. We are also free to accept the consequences of our decisions. It is a good thing to stay inside boundaries.

HOW?

More than likely, you already know most of the boundaries you need to keep in your youth ministry. Just in case, here are some personal and professional boundaries I suggest you set to safeguard your ministry.

Take your day off and vacation. Take the time you have been given. For more information on this boundary, read Self-Care Matters.

Do not let your cell phone interrupt life. When possible, turn your phone off or silence notifications when talking with people (especially your spouse and kids). Avoid posting everything you see immediately to social media (you can post later). Live in the moment.

Do not skip date night. If you are single and it is a night with friends or if you are married and a night with your spouse is the plan, don't skip the occasion. Nothing is more important than your key relationships.

Protect your home. Youth ministers are notorious for making their homes open and available for teenage traffic twenty-four seven. While an environment of openness comes with the job, it is imperative (married or single, kids or no kids) that you tell students it's time to leave or set up hours of acceptable non-emergency drop-in times. Especially when you have kids, protect the time you have with just you or your family.

Do not communicate with students after 10:30 P.M. Yes, you may react to a social media post of a student, but late-night responses to personal messages are creepy. From a parent's perspective, it better be a pretty urgent matter to break this boundary.

Tell the truth. This should never be an issue with a youth minister. This includes inflating successes and credentials as well.

Take responsibility. It is easy to take responsibility when things go well in your ministry and life, but take responsibility for and accept the consequences of failures as well.

Keep physical contact way above reproach. Stay away from the full-body embrace. Side hugs rule! Lap sitting, cuddling, sharing blankets, kisses, or any "this is creepy" contact must be avoided. If you are a touchy-feely youth minister and have no idea what inappropriate contact is, ask someone to tell you. Yes, students need appropriate physical contact from adults. Even so, way above reproach is the goal in today's world.

Never be alone with a student. Keep office doors open or within glass-pane viewing when with a student. Meet in coffee shops or other public spaces. Never be alone with a student in their house, especially their bedroom. Never be alone with a student in a van or camp dorm room. The point is to be seen and accountable with students. Be sure there are other people in the office or building area when visiting with a student.

Practice the two-adult rule. When transporting a student, male or female, have another adult with you on the trip. If possible, never travel alone with a student. If unaccompanied travel is unavoidable, be sure people know your exact itinerary and timetable.

Do not travel with a coworker of the opposite sex. Full-time or intern, do not run errands, visit a teenager, or make a drive-through run with a member of the opposite sex. It may seem rather strict, but it is a great above-reproach practice.

Do not talk about personal issues with students. Do not use teenagers as your sounding board for working through relationship, ministry, coworker, or other struggles. Find an adult friend to process difficulties.

Do not talk down about church leadership. It is easy to get caught up in a conversation and begin to gossip and tear down church leadership. There may be times when conflict-related and sensitive information needs to be addressed and processed with a church leader, trusted coworker, or volunteer. If that is the case, choose your words wisely, and assume that whatever you say will be repeated.

Most of us know the boundaries we need to observe in order to survive the long haul of youth ministry, but knowing and doing are two different things.

NOW?

We all have a little kid inside of us that likes to color outside the lines at times. There is nothing wrong with that tendency when it comes to creativity and vision. However, when boundaries are concerned, you must commit yourself to coloring inside the lines.

Decide now to prepare before. Yes, an intentionally awkward sentence so you will remember to make the decision to live with boundaries. Occupants of old castles built surrounding walls because they knew an attack would eventually come. You will be tested. Be prepared.[1]

Identify weaknesses. As you read through the list of recommended boundaries, did you discover a weak boundary area? It may be helpful to go through these boundaries with your spouse or trusted friend. Let them evaluate the strength of each boundary.

Fix and strengthen your boundaries. We all have weaknesses in a boundary area that need improvement. Do the work of making your boundaries stronger (accountability is a great tool in strengthening your weak areas).

Seek professional guidance. If commitment and accountability don't do the job of helping you determine and live within set boundaries, you may need to turn to a professional. A professional counselor can help you identify the origins of why you continue to live outside boundaries and/or help you establish strong boundaries.

"David, I am concerned because you are a hugger."

I never really thought of this as a problem for my youth ministry until a concerned youth minister (who was dealing with the consequences resulting from a crossed barrier) reached out to me for a visit. After explaining his own failure, he cared enough about me, my marriage, and my ministry to let me know that he was concerned my "huggy" nature was eventually going to cause me problems if I did not establish strong boundaries.

So, I listened to him and strengthened my boundaries.

Even though awkward at the time, I am thankful for this man's courage and transparency. He felt the need to visit because he had learned this lesson the hard way.

CONCLUDING TRUTH: BOUNDARIES MATTER.

BUDGETS
MATTER

"You are going to have to slow down the spending!"

The summer was over and we still had nine months of programming to get through before a new budget year. Yikes!

My administrative assistant was the best I had ever worked with in this area. She had a gift for budgets and finances, which is a blessing for a youth minister. As the words were spoken, I knew we were in a precarious situation. Did I mention we were a few weeks away from our all-campus youth retreat? Yikes, indeed!

"Honey, we have ended up using the credit card at the end of each month for a while now. We have to stop the spending!"

This is always a fun conversation starter with my wife. To be clear, I do not buy a lot of stuff, but I do love to go out to eat with friends and students and pay for lunches. Well, you should not do that if you have no money. But I often do, and I often get sucked into the "I will pay this off later" trap. When you live on a tight budget, there is not a lot of wiggle room for overspending (even when done with great intentions).

Did either one of these stories cause the hairs on the back of your neck to stand on end? If so, whether you have been in either of these situations or not, you know.

TRUTH: BUDGETS MATTER.

WHY?

Large or small, all the money and resources we have been given to use and manage belong to the Lord. We need to manage them well. The Scriptures have a lot to say about money.

> Dishonest money dwindles away, but whoever gathers money little by little makes it grow (Prov. 13:11).

> Whoever loves money never has enough; whoever loves wealth is never satisfied with their income. This too is meaningless (Eccles. 5:10).

> No one can serve two masters. Either you will hate the one and love the other, or you will be devoted to the one and despise the other. You cannot serve both God and money (Matt. 6:24).

> So he called ten of his servants and gave them ten minas. "Put this money to work," he said, "until I come back" (Luke 19:13).

> For the love of money is a root of all kinds of evil. Some people, eager for money, have wandered from the faith and pierced themselves with many griefs (1 Tim. 6:10).

> Keep your lives free from the love of money and be content with what you have, because God has

said, "Never will I leave you; never will I forsake you"
(Heb. 13:5).

Every good and perfect gift is from above, coming
down from the Father of the heavenly lights, who
does not change like shifting shadows (James 1:17).

When reading the Gospels, you will notice the use and management of money come up often in Jesus's interaction with people.
Why? Jesus gave us that answer. "For where your treasure is,
there your heart will be also" (Matt. 6:21). At the end of the day,
our ability or inability to use and manage money and resources
is directly connected to our heart. Again, yikes!

That is why the mismanagement of church and personal
budgets has the potential to become intense, emotional, and
frustrating (and can end up getting you fired).

The ability to manage money and resources is a *big deal*.

HOW?

Youth ministers are not accountants. Some youthworkers may
have come out of the finance management or accounting world,
but many youthworkers have never taken a money management class. Even so, the ability to manage money and resources
is necessary to be successful in youth ministry.

As you can see from the introduction, I am not perfect in
my professional and personal budgeting. I have learned a few
things that can help you quick-start your budgeting adventure.

Ask for help and training. Sit down with your church accountant, trusted minister, or finance-savvy volunteer (accountant,
investor, banker, etc.), and get educated on the basics of personal and professional budgeting. Be ready. More than likely,
they will ask you questions concerning cost of activities, number

of participants, scholarship participants, cost of transportation, etc. In other words, you may end up with more questions than answers. Great. At least you will be given a direction and know what to ask the next time you meet.

Do not spend more than you have been given. This is so obvious, but as you read in the beginning of this chapter, this knowledge does not always stop the spending. If a decision to overspend is strategically made,[1] decide where the money is going to be transferred from to account for the overage.

Own and explain overages. Whether for strategic, explainable reasons or because of clear mismanagement, quickly own and explain budgeting mistakes. And, work to keep your defensiveness down and your humility up, promising to learn from the situation.

Be careful with outsourcing your responsibility. Even if you are blessed to have an administrative assistant who loves and is gifted in the budgeting aspect of ministry, you need to be aware and educate yourself. Ultimately, it is you who will be held accountable for your budget. This also holds true for your personal or family budget.

Know the numbers. Know how much things cost! Know how many participants are projected to participate. It takes intentional, strategic planning to know.

Work from a real budget. Do not simply ask for an increase every year; know why you need an increase. Not knowing does not work in your personal or professional budgets. More than likely, your church will outline your budget process. If not, start with your mission statement and your program to fulfill that mission. If you have no idea where to start for budgeting the youth ministry, go back to the first quick-start suggestion of asking for training and help.

Report the wins. What you count indicates what you value. What you value is what you budget to achieve. Read those two sentences again, and you will know the importance of accurate record keeping (How many students attended? How many adults served? How many decisions for Christ?) and storytelling (How many stories of change and buy-in can you tell?). It is nearly impossible to get a budget increase when you cannot demonstrate the need.

It can be a challenge managing youth ministry money and resources. Following the above quick-start suggestions will help you work through that challenge.

NOW?

Budgeting may be something you put off to the last possible minute. If that is the case, then changing that is the first step. Get on top of managing your money and resources today.

Inventory. Do you know how much money you have in your budget? Do you know when you spend the bulk of your money? Do you know if you are asking for enough money from your participants? Find out. Do you know what is in your youth ministry closet(s)? Find out. The point here is to get a baseline of your current money and resources.

Record keeping. If you do not already have a system of receipt accountability and reporting in place, get one quickly. No idea what system should be in place? Go back to the first quick-start suggestion of asking for training and help.

Budgeting. Make your next budget (yearly, monthly, or event-specific) the most accurate and reliable guide yet for your allotted youth ministry money and resources. It takes time and effort, but is worth it.

"We want you to increase the amount of money you have in your summer camp budget item."

That was great news to hear from my supervisor. Our camp participation numbers had continued to grow, and the over-age in our budget was well-documented and defendable. We worked the process of knowing the numbers and reporting the wins.

It would have been easy to get frustrated along the way. The budgeting process is not the most enjoyable, but it can be most rewarding if done with excellence and strategic purpose.

CONCLUDING TRUTH: BUDGETS MATTER.

THE CHURCH
MATTERS

"I got into youth ministry because I don't like working with adults!"

I am shocked every time I hear a youth minister speak some form of this statement. In my experience, these words are usually spoken by "rock star" youth ministers who love drawing a crowd. The problem with such crowds is that they mostly consist of cool and younger adult volunteer groupies who share their leader's harmful opinion.

I understand the draw of developing an attractive youth ministry program. As a matter of fact, several of these types of youth ministries seem to be doing rather well with their exclusively teen Sunday worship services and state-of-the-art youth centers. They do draw the crowds, but be careful of how you measure success.

Adult involvement is a key factor in measuring youth ministry success. In fact, adults are one of the main reasons students stay involved with the church after graduation.[1] Intergenerational Sunday worship opportunities are a huge factor in fostering that future involvement. Therefore, even though it has the potential to draw a crowd, diminishing adult involvement and contact with students diminishes the likelihood that students will remain connected to faith after high school.[2] To be most effective, youth ministers need to work to get the entire congregation involved in youth ministry.

This statement irritates me: "Our teenagers are the church of tomorrow." To be fair, I have not heard that statement in a long while, and I am glad. Why does this statement irritate me? Because our students are very much the church of today, and their role in the Body of Christ is welcomed.

TRUTH: THE CHURCH MATTERS.

 WHY?

Teenagers are part of the church. As such, youth ministry programming should be carried out in the context of the wider church community. Within this community, so much of what a teenager wants and needs is provided.

> Just as a body, though one, has many parts, but all its many parts form one body, so it is with Christ. For we were all baptized by one Spirit so as to form one body—whether Jews or Gentiles, slave or free—and we were all given the one Spirit to drink. Even so the body is not made up of one part but of many. . . . But in fact God has placed the parts in the body, every one of them, just as he wanted them to be. If they were all one part, where would the body be? As it is, there are many parts, but one body. The eye cannot say to the hand, "I don't need you!" And the head cannot say to the feet, "I don't need you!" On the contrary, those parts of the body that seem to be weaker

are indispensable, and the parts that we think are less honorable we treat with special honor. And the parts that are unpresentable are treated with special modesty, while our presentable parts need no special treatment. But God has put the body together, giving greater honor to the parts that lacked it, so that there should be no division in the body, but that its parts should have equal concern for each other. If one part suffers, every part suffers with it; if one part is honored, every part rejoices with it (1 Cor. 12:12–14, 18–26).

I have included this rather long passage for a reason. Slow down and read this section of Scripture again. Notice that inclusion, purpose, value, and support are themes that run through Paul's discussion on the church. These are all qualities that a teenager wants and needs and that can be found in the community of the church.

Teach the older men to be temperate, worthy of respect, self-controlled, and sound in faith, in love and in endurance. Likewise, teach the older women to be reverent in the way they live, not to be slanderers or addicted to much wine, but to teach what is good. Then they can urge the younger women to love their husbands and children, to be self-controlled and pure, to be busy at home, to be kind, and to be subject to their husbands, so that no one will malign the word of God. Similarly, encourage the young men to be self-controlled. In everything set them an example by doing what is good. In your teaching show integrity, seriousness and soundness of speech that cannot be condemned, so that those who oppose

you may be ashamed because they have nothing bad
to say about us (Titus 2:2–8).

When Paul spoke to Titus concerning the teaching of appropriate doctrine, young and old were intentionally mentioned
together. He expected the young and old to be in dynamic
relationship within the church in order to ensure that a holy
lifestyle was maintained.

To be clear, I am not advocating we shut down youth ministry programming. On the contrary, there is great benefit found
in letting each generation process, challenge, educate, and find
support within their own peer groups. However, this should
not be done at the exclusion of intergenerational connection.

Because age-specific programming draws a crowd, it is difficult to see why exclusively separating age groups for ministry
programming is a bad idea. To be fair, each age group is getting
their needs met on their own level. That is good. Right?

Let's take a two-question quiz:

* How many sermons, lessons, and programming
  moments (camp, retreat, conference, etc.) do you
  remember that impacted your spiritual life?
* How many adult relationships do you remember that
  impacted your spiritual life?

I am certain that you can recall more people than programs. It's
not that youth ministry programming is inconsequential, but
you probably remember adults who made those programs so
impactful and memorable.

Yes, sometimes the church body needs homogenous connection events. Nonetheless, do not underestimate the power of
integrating your students into church-wide programming and
using large numbers of multigenerational adults as volunteers

in your youth ministry. Teenagers are part of the church, and the church plays a part in youth ministry programming.

HOW?

It is easier to draw a crowd of teenagers to a dodgeball tournament than to a Sunday morning worship service or Bible class with adults. If numbers are the only measure, then we should not work to integrate youth ministry programming into the entire church context. However, you know (and hopefully your church leadership knows) that spiritual growth is more important than the ability to draw crowds of happy teenagers. You know your students will graduate from youth ministry one day, but you do not want them to graduate from church. Here are some tips to better integrate students into the church body:

Expand your volunteer youthworker pool. Make it possible for any qualified adult to serve in your youth ministry. Some of the greatest volunteers I have worked with in youth ministry were neither college students nor parents of a teenager. They were professionals or retired persons who were willing to be an authentic presence in a student's life.

Tell stories. Invite the older members of your church into your youth ministry classes to tell their stories on what it was like to be a teenager, about what has been the greatest challenge in their walk with Jesus, and to share words of wisdom with your teenagers.

Integrate. If you believe your teenagers are the church of today, then integrate them into the *normal life* of the church body. Get them serving in the classroom, worship service, and work days. Get them involved with church leadership projects or teams. Stop applauding them for short-term mission or service efforts.

Instead, mention their work alongside that of the entire church family. Stop applauding them when they learn a new ministry skill. Instead, plug that skill into the ministry of the church. This suggestion may get you to throw this book, but have your teens stop sitting together in the "youth group section." Spread out among the church.

Collaborate. Visit with other ministers on your staff and key church leaders about ways the youth ministry can best integrate into the entire church body. You are the youth minister and missionary to teen culture, so collaborate with your church on creative ways in which adults and teenagers can be meaningfully involved in church life together.

Work together. Find opportunities in which adults and teenagers can work together. These can include short-term mission trips, cleaning a yard, prepping for a church-wide event, teaching, worship leading, preaching, working on a widow's car, etc. Use your imagination and make use of the collaboration you have done. Get your students working with the church body as co-laborers. They will give life to your community.

Worship together. This is so simple but is extremely profound in a teenager's life. If you are at a church that separates the students and adults during weekly worship, explore and make use of the information available in *Sticky Faith* by Kara E. Powell and Chap Clark, and start the process of integrating your students into the assembly. If your students are integrated but the worship is anything but inspiring, patiently work with your ministry staff to revitalize the assembly. Change is a painfully slow process, so be responsible with your words. Your teenagers are watching how you handle conflict.

The church is the institution the Lord has chosen to bless the world and bring support to his followers. Since the church is filled with people, it has its difficulties. But keep in mind what Jesus told the apostle Peter after his confession:

> "And I tell you that you are Peter, and on this rock I will build my church, and the gates of Hades will not overcome it" (Matt. 16:18).

If you want to build a youth ministry that storms the gates of Hades, you better be sure that youth ministry is tucked firmly within the ministry of the church.

 ## NOW?

Youth ministers agree that the church matters in youth ministry. The challenge comes when ministers focus on integrating youth ministry and church-wide ministry programming. Conflict is to be expected. Not everyone, young or old, wants their silo of ministry activity disturbed. So how do you proceed?

Communicate the need. Use the information in this chapter and the Relationships Matter chapter to communicate the need and importance of church in every Christian's life. A church-wide class or sermon series would be ideal.

Relieve stress. Let your church know that age-specific programming is important and should not be devalued.

Change something. It does not need to be big, but it needs to be significant. Perhaps the youth group can stop sitting together during worship, or the students can join an adult service project or game night at church. Have a group of senior adults join your youth group and share their stories.

Repeat. Keep going. Be focused and determined that when your students leave your ministry, they will not only have a strong connection to the youth program but to the church body as well.

✿

"Will you join our family for Senior Sunday?"

Senior Sunday is a special event in many youth ministries. It is a time when we honor, say goodbye, and bless graduating high school seniors.

John had come to our church in the fourth grade. John's mother, an incredible woman, knew she needed to find a community of faith that would support and encourage her family. She was losing her husband, had a special needs child who took a lot of her time, and had a young son who needed male role models. John was placed on my Upwards football team, and soon he and his mother became members of our church family.

John was involved in every aspect of our youth ministry and integrated beautifully into the entire church body. Now, at the end of his time with our youth ministry, his mom made the request for me to join her and the rest of John's "family" for his graduation blessing. Joining me in this special blessing circle was his track coach, another young family, and his special-needs sister. I quickly noticed that I was the only "official" connection to the youth ministry program. The church had showed up, and it was beautiful.

John, his mother, and his sister were not only impacted by the youth ministry but by the entire church body.

CONCLUDING TRUTH: THE CHURCH MATTERS.

COMMUNICATION
MATTERS

"Shout-out to the old man in the back!"

Many years ago, when looking for a better way to teach practical morality to teenagers, I came up with my five-finger lesson—a lesson in which every finger represents a scripture and corresponding truth that is easy to recall when facing a moral dilemma. It worked. I have taught that lesson many times throughout the years. It still works and is easy for students (and adults) to recall.

I was visiting a youth ministry I had once worked with, and the youth minister was reading a statement from a senior student. The student's statement was advice they would give underclassmen. Their advice was, "Surround yourself with good people."

The much younger youth minister who had taken my place immediately realized the origin of the student's comment and said, "Shout-out to the old man in the back!" While not excited about the truth of the old man comment, the student's comments provided a moment of great affirmation. A student had recalled and shared content from a youth ministry teaching.

TRUTH: COMMUNICATION MATTERS.

WHY?

Communication is powerful. Communication has the power to create or destroy, bring order or chaos, bring peace or division.

> And God said, "Let there be light," and there was light (Gen. 1:3).

> Fix these words of mine in your hearts and minds; tie them as symbols on your hands and bind them on your foreheads (Deut. 11:18).

> His talk is smooth as butter, yet war is in his heart; his words are more soothing than oil, yet they are drawn swords (Ps. 55:21).

> The unfolding of your words gives light; it gives understanding to the simple (Ps. 119:130).

> Then he taught me, and he said to me, "Take hold of my words with all your heart; keep my commands, and you will live" (Prov. 4:4).

> With persuasive words she led him astray; she seduced him with her smooth talk (Prov. 7:21).

> Gracious words are a honeycomb, sweet to the soul and healing to the bones (Prov. 16:24).

> And because of his words many more became believers (John 4:41).

> The Spirit gives life; the flesh counts for nothing. The
> words I have spoken to you—they are full of the
> Spirit and life (John 6:63).

> Keep reminding God's people of these things. Warn
> them before God against quarreling about words;
> it is of no value, and only ruins those who listen
> (2 Tim. 2:14).

Verbal or nonverbal, subtle or direct, communication is something everyone does every day. We cannot avoid communicating—it is what we do. We are communicators.

As a result, even when attempting to be noncommunicative, we are bombarded by the communication of others. From televisions, cell phones (and all that goes with that platform), computers, radios, movies, billboards, and flyers to banners being flown from airplanes, we are flooded daily by waves of communication.

With so many words being spoken, a youth minister has to work to assure his communication is being heard.

HOW?

Most youth ministers are natural communicators, but not necessarily extroverted. Introverts can be effective youth ministers and excellent communicators as well. Do not make the mistake of thinking that either extroversion or introversion has an edge for effective communication. Both youth ministry personality types have the responsibility to ensure that effective communication is happening in their ministry. Below are a few tips that will help youth ministers become more effective communicators of both their programming and message delivery.

Programming. Parents and students need to receive clear and accurate information on youth ministry programming if you want them to be involved. We have all complained about it, but the busy pace of today's family demands effective communication. This need will not change.

Six-month rule. Parents and students need to know what you want them to plan for, regarding both time and money, at least six months in advance. Anything less will cause anxiousness and frustration.

Uniformity. Websites, social media platforms, flyers, slide templates, and other forms of communication should have a unified look that brands youth ministry programming and connects youth programming with the overall church ministry. This reduces clutter, and it lets your audience know the communication is coming from your ministry.

Clarity. Be sure that you are clearly communicating who, what, when, where, how, and why messages. Yes, grammar and spelling counts. Proofreading is not optional.

Communication channels. Websites, texting, Instagram, emails, letters, flyers, posters, cards, banners, slide templates, videos, songs, and more are all usable channels of communication. Find what works for you, and be willing to change channels when your message is no longer being heard.

Finding the sweet spot. It is important to determine the amount of communication needed to push your message to the front of a flooded message market. We all get those emails that we automatically delete because we just do not have time to read them. It is possible to communicate too much. Find the balance that ensures your message is being delivered.

Above reproach. Even with your best attempt at communicating, you will receive this message from a parent or teen: "I did not know about that." Again, this is unavoidable. In such situations, be sure you can respond with, "Did you receive the parent email, text, or flyer, or hear the announcement in class?"

Seasonal meetings. No one likes to attend a nonproductive meeting with an agenda that could have been communicated by email. Even though some of your veteran parents and students may feel this way, seasonal programming meetings (fall meetings in August or September and spring meetings in January or February) are excellent ways to make sure your programming is clearly communicated. This is also a great time to once again communicate your mission statement and your philosophy of youth ministry.

Message Delivery. Youth ministers are called upon to communicate in all kinds of situations. The most obvious are teaching, preaching, and leading ministry meetings. You may also be called upon to host a conference, deliver announcements in the assembly, or conduct a wedding or funeral. As a minister, the ability to communicate is expected. Here are some tips for delivering an effective message:

Confident. You have done your study and understand the content, so there is no reason to let nerves get the best of your presentation. Be confident. Confidence in a speaker is quickly determined by an audience often within the first few moments of a communication. A strong voice (not necessarily loud) and a quick move from the takeoff into the lesson or presentation exude confidence. However, nervous chatter ("let me find my place," "I lost my place," and "hmm" are all examples) or downplaying your abilities ("I am not the real preacher," "I don't normally do this," or "I am the fill-in and hope I share something good" statements) have the ability to quickly derail effective communication and take the audience's confidence away.

Articulate. Speak up and pronounce words clearly and accurately. If needed, practice saying difficult words out loud.

Passionate. Does your audience know the content you are sharing is important to you? Yes, it is hard to be passionate about delivering the church announcements. But even in that moment of communication, you can be passionate about what is going on in your church community.

Speed of delivery. Be careful of the speed in which you are communicating your message. Too fast and your audience may not be able to keep up; too slow and your audience may get tired of listening.

Concise. Audiences do not need to be impressed with how smart you are. They will know quickly how well you know your content. Your content should be given in chunks and phrases that are easy to follow, understandable, and most important, applicable to their lives. If the content is especially complex, it is difficult to compress content into concise morsels of truth. Do the hard work.

Creative. Most youth ministers love to be creative when they communicate. A video, song, group activity, onstage demonstration, prop, or drama presentation are a few of the many creative avenues available for communication. Don't lose focus on your intended message as you dream up creative ways to deliver that message.

Takeoff and landing. It is imperative that you nail the first and last moments of your message. The takeoff is that opening statement, question, or illustration that draws your audience into your message. You are helping the audience answer the question, "Why do I need to listen?" The landing is that closing statement, question, or illustration that calls your audience to action. You are helping the audience answer the question, "What do I need to do with this message?"

There will always be the temptation to pattern your communication style after that of your favorite communicator. You will certainly pick up various communication tips from other people, but commit yourself to becoming the best communicator you can be.

 NOW?
There is a message that you are getting ready to communicate. Commit to be the best communicator you can be in each of these situations.

Evaluate programming communication. By yourself or with your youth ministry team, evaluate the effectiveness of program communication.

* Are church members getting the messages your ministry is delivering? Why or why not?
* Are visitors getting the messages your ministry is delivering? Why or why not?

* What can or needs to be changed to better communicate youth ministry programming? (Make use of the
  suggestions given.)

Evaluate message delivery communication. By yourself or
with a trusted mentor (fellow youth minister, minister, or
friend), evaluate the effectiveness of your message delivery.
This can be rough, but it's needed every so often to assure you
are growing as a communicator.

* Ask your trusted mentor to listen to one of your
  messages (live or recorded) and provide feedback.
  Share with them the above suggestions as a template
  for evaluation.
* Listen to a past message you have given and do a self-
  evaluation of your effectiveness.
* Watch a video or listen to a podcast of a speaker you
  consider to be an effective communicator. What makes
  him or her effective? Is there something you can
  implement in your own communication?

Keep growing. Evaluation is tough and personal. Don't be dis-
couraged. No one is a perfect communicator. Keep growing.
And be sure to read the Teaching Matters chapter for further
quick-start suggestions.

"You will never guess what I am sharing in chapel today."

I went to visit an old youth group student who serves as
the spiritual life director at a local Christian school. As we were
concluding our conversation, he called me to his computer
screen so I could see what he was working on for chapel.

He was reproducing (and improving) a lesson I had given many years ago when he was a teenager.

I was blown away that he had remembered and honored that he felt it worthy to share with his own students. And, I was reminded once again of the power of communication.

CONCLUDING TRUTH: COMMUNICATION MATTERS.

CONFLICT MATTERS

"I am going to have to take this to the elders!"

I was so frustrated and done with what I perceived to be a series of petty complaints that I welcomed the opportunity to stand before our church leaders in defense of my actions.

The great, dark, ugly sin I was guilty of embracing? I would not stop leading 4/4 time signature worship songs in 2/4 time! Fun fact. Technically, it is permissible to lead a 4/4 song in 2/4 time.

If you are not from an a cappella tradition, you may not see the great offense. In short, the leader in voices-only traditions typically uses his or her arms like a conductor to lead the audience in worship. Without drums and acoustic guitars, the leader is responsible for starting, stopping, and keeping everyone on the same beat to create that beautiful a cappella sound. The time signature determines the movement pattern of the leader.

In the leader's opinion, I was breaking the time signature movement pattern law. Therefore, I was not following the scriptural command that ". . . everything should be done in a fitting and orderly way" (1 Cor. 14:40). I am not making this stuff up! How I wish I was, but this really happened. So, following the teachings of Jesus in Matthew 18:15–19 (yes, he used this passage), he asked to meet with me one-on-one. And I did not change my "law breaking." He met with me a second time and informed me that "many had witnessed my offense" (yes, another misapplication of Scripture). And I did not change my "law breaking." His last step was to report me to the elders of our church as an unrepentant sinner.

The next week, I attended the elders' meeting. At the end of the meeting, the tone of the room shifted to somber as the chairman handed me an envelope and asked me to open it in the presence of everyone in the room. It was an intimidating moment. For a moment, I really thought I was about to be fired for my unwillingness to repent from inappropriate worship leading. The message inside the envelope, written on a certificate, read: "Congratulations on surviving John! Welcome to the ministry, David!"

The elders broke into laughter, followed by affirmation of my ministry and recognition that they had dealt with and would continue to deal with this man's immaturity. After catching my breath, I had a great laugh and was instructed by my leaders that conflict, large or small, is a constant in ministry. This event happened over twenty-eight years ago. I agree. Conflict is a constant.

TRUTH: CONFLICT MATTERS.

WHY?

You cannot avoid it. Conflict will find you in youth ministry. You are working with people and their kids, which provides an extremely rich conflict environment. Prepare yourself to productively work through the conflict.

Why all the conflict? The Scriptures give us a lot of insight.

Then the LORD said to Cain, "Why are you angry? Why is your face downcast? If you do what is right, will you not be accepted? But if you do not do what is right, sin is crouching at your door; it desires to have you, but you must rule over it" (Gen. 4:6–7).

A gentle answer turns away wrath, but a harsh word stirs up anger (Prov. 15:1).

A perverse person stirs up conflict, and a gossip separates close friends (Prov. 16:28).

They [Paul and Barnabas] had such a sharp disagreement that they parted company (Acts 15:39a).

Live in harmony with one another. Do not be proud, but be willing to associate with people of low position. Do not be conceited (Rom. 12:16).

For the flesh desires what is contrary to the Spirit, and the Spirit what is contrary to the flesh. They are in conflict with each other, so that you are not to do whatever you want (Gal. 5:17).

What causes fights and quarrels among you? Don't they come from your desires that battle within you? You desire but do not have, so you kill. You covet but you cannot get what you want, so you quarrel and fight. You do not have because you do not ask God. When you ask, you do not receive, because you ask with wrong motives, that you may spend what you get on your pleasures (James 4:1–3).

Jealousy, anger, gossip, disagreements, arrogance, and fleshly desires are all seen in these passages. Youth ministers will see similar types of conflict in their ministries.

"Why did that kid get selected and not mine?"
"They said something hateful toward me!"
"I heard that they were drinking!"
"I just can't work with them anymore!"
"I do not want my kid around those types of kids!"
"They are doing things in that house that are just wrong!"
"They get everything they want. It's not fair!"

I have heard and been in the middle of each of these conflict situations, all unavoidable but manageable. Actually, even though it may take time, discomfort, and pain, everyone involved in a conflict situation can grow and learn from the experience. "As iron sharpens iron, so one person sharpens another" (Prov. 27:17). Sparks may fly, but everyone is sharpened by the process of conflict resolution. And resolution[1] is what the Father expects from his children.

Therefore, if you are offering your gift at the altar and there remember that your brother or sister has something against you, leave your gift there in front of the altar. First go and be reconciled to them; then come and offer your gift (Matt. 5:23–24).

We love because he first loved us. Whoever claims to love God yet hates a brother or sister is a liar. For whoever does not love their brother and sister, whom they have seen, cannot love God, whom they have not seen. And he has given us this command:

> Anyone who loves God must also love their brother
> and sister (1 John 4:19–21).

Because I know myself and what is in my heart when in conflict, I keep the apostle John's words close to my heart in difficult situations with coworkers, parents, or students. Do you remember Jesus's somewhat confusing words in the Sermon on the Mount? "Be perfect, therefore, as your heavenly Father is perfect" (Matt. 5:48). Go back and look at the context. These words were spoken at the end of several difficult relationship teachings, and specifically in the context of loving our enemies. Enemies! The Father's perfect love is witnessed in sacrifice. He expects the same from us. It matters how we handle conflict.

HOW?

Youth ministry conflicts can and should be managed to a productive conclusion. In my opinion, there are two things that are basic to learning how to manage conflict. First, youth ministers need to believe in, commit to, and want to work toward the ideal. As the apostle Paul said to the conflicted Corinthian church:

> I appeal to you, brothers and sisters, in the name
> of our Lord Jesus Christ, that all of you agree with
> one another in what you say and that there be no
> divisions among you, but that you be perfectly united
> in mind and thought (1 Cor. 1:10).

> Finally, brothers and sisters, rejoice! Strive for full
> restoration, encourage one another, be of one mind,
> live in peace. And the God of love and peace will be
> with you (2 Cor. 13:11).

"Appeal" and "strive" are two powerful words used in the context of conflict. These are good words for youth ministers to remember in today's church environment.

Second, youth ministers should follow the teachings of Jesus and his followers when faced with a conflict situation. This is not an exhaustive list, but look at the wisdom given in these scriptures:

> If your brother or sister sins, go and point out their fault, just between the two of you. If they listen to you, you have won them over. But if they will not listen, take one or two others along, so that "every matter may be established by the testimony of two or three witnesses." If they still refuse to listen, tell it to the church; and if they refuse to listen even to the church, treat them as you would a pagan or a tax collector. Truly I tell you, whatever you bind on earth will be bound in heaven, and whatever you loose on earth will be loosed in heaven. Again, truly I tell you that if two of you on earth agree about anything they ask for, it will be done for them by my Father in heaven. For where two or three gather in my name, there am I with them (Matt. 18:15–20).

> My dear brothers and sisters, take note of this: Everyone should be quick to listen, slow to speak and slow to become angry, because human anger does not produce the righteousness that God desires (James 1:19–20).

> Brothers and sisters, if someone is caught in a sin, you who live by the Spirit should restore that person

gently. But watch yourselves, or you also may be tempted. Carry each other's burdens, and in this way you will fulfill the law of Christ. If anyone thinks they are something when they are not, they deceive themselves. Each one should test their own actions. Then they can take pride in themselves alone, without comparing themselves to someone else, for each one should carry their own load (Gal. 6:1–5).

Sin is the presenting issue in two of these scriptures, and is often a factor in conflict. Still, systematic advice for handling interpersonal conflict is helpful in several situations. There are resources you can turn to for education and guidance when facing conflict.[2]

It is possible that you are reading this chapter because you are in the middle of a conflict right now. If so, this is not an exhaustive list, but here are a few suggestions.

Minimizing conflict. The key to minimizing (or avoiding) conflict is communication.

Communicate expectations clearly. Conflicts can quickly arise when this does not happen. For example, if you send a student home early from a mission trip for breaking curfew, you better have placed that expectation in writing and have communicated that during the pre-trip meeting. A conflict with that student's parents is all but guaranteed, but going back and highlighting the communicated expectation will minimize the tension. Whatever the expectation, communicate clearly.

Communicate process clearly. Feelings can be hurt, and conflict often follows when processes are not clearly communicated. For example, if a student is not chosen for the praise team, tension can be reduced by clearly communicating the process by which students will be judged and chosen before the actual audition. Auditions (drama team, praise team, leadership teams, etc.), participation qualifications (age, grade, fitness level, etc.), program changes (trip dates, removal or addition of programming, etc.), and other potential conflict-inducing situations can be minimized by communicating process clearly.

Communicate failure quickly. If it is your fault, claim it. Covering up and rationalizing mistakes heightens conflict in your ministry. We live in a contentious culture, and there will be moments when you will need to consult your leaders before confessing your fault. If in doubt, reach out!

Working through conflict. Several of the suggestions below originated from the scriptures mentioned above and the list of resources given in the notes. I have used all of these in my years of working with students, parents, coworkers, and employees.

Set the environment. If a conflict erupts during or on the way to an event (conflict in a church van etc.), you have no choice but to secure the environment and get the conflicting parties away from the group to process the situation. If at all possible, have a trusted adult witness the conflict management process in those erupting situations. Whenever possible, have the conflicting party or parties join you in your office or location that is conducive for uninterrupted conversation.

Pray. Always give your time to the Lord. As Matthew 18:20 tells us, Jesus joins us in conflict mediation.[3]

Remain calm. This is your leverage and strength in conflict. Even if you are being yelled at, remain calm. Your calmness will lower the tension and give the best opportunity for your words to be heard. Without control, everyone will be on the offensive in being defensive.

Listen before you speak. When challenged, it is natural to stop listening and begin formulating a response. Fight this natural urge. If mediating conflict, assure that each party can speak their side of the story with respect and without interruption.

Be aware of triangulation. When out of balance, it is human to reach out for something that can restore balance (e.g., you are falling and throw out an arm to catch yourself). Conflict creates imbalance, and most reach out to another person in an attempt to restore balance. Hopefully, such a reach will result in wise counsel (a family member, friend, or leader). However, a reach-out can result in unhealthy partnerships with unwise and toxic people who have nothing to do with the conflict and love being in the middle. Also, beware of unhealthy activities or substances. Being aware of who or what is being angled for balance will help you understand the real origin of and the players in the conflict.[4]

Talk to, not around, the issue. Do not beat around the bush. It may be uncomfortable, but speak directly to the issue. For instance, if you are about to tell a parent that their child had sex on a retreat (going for a severely uncomfortable situation here), tell them exactly what you know.

Talk to, not around, those involved. Recalling the need for "triangle" awareness, be sure you are meeting with those directly involved with the conflict. You may have to make a judgment call for those wanting their friends with them for support, but typically, the best conflict work happens when meeting with those directly involved in the situation.

Work toward resolution. If possible, find a collaborative solution (win-win) to the conflict. This type of resolution comes from all parties accepting their responsibility in the conflict and resulting solution. A compromised solution (win-loss) takes the same type of responsibility, but involves one or both parties conceding (losing) something. If a resolution is not possible, a withdrawal of conflict should be agreed upon until another meeting can be arranged.[5]

Restate the resolution and next steps. If one has been reached, summarize the resolution and each party's responsibility (next steps) to assure that resolution is followed.

Take and keep notes. Shortly after the meeting, record the who, what, when, where, and how of the conflict. Keep those notes in a secure file location. This will provide a valuable resource if or when a conflict flares up or expands to legal action.

Know your conflict style. Youth ministers need to know how they typically conduct themselves in a conflict situation. Do you avoid conflict? Do you go into combat mode when challenged? You can find your style by taking one of several available inventories.[6] By the way, pay particular attention to your second-highest conflict style. We turn to our second when unable to use the first.

An angry parent is waiting for you at your office. Your senior minister is asking for a meeting in his office. A fistfight broke out in the middle of a mission trip, and one of the students has a broken nose. You are not alone. No youth minister enjoys the burden of an upcoming conflict. Take a deep breath, pray, and step into the conflict.

NOW?

It is possible you may have a conflict literally waiting outside your door or hanging out in your inbox or voicemail to handle. If so, review the above suggestions and get ready to step into the situation with confidence. When the crisis has passed and you have a moment, spend time on the following questions:

Do you find yourself in the middle of conflict often? I do not want to be difficult, but I do want you to be prepared. So I am going to push in on both sides of this answer.

* If the answer is "no," is it because you are doing a great job of minimizing conflict? Or are you passively avoiding conflict?

* If the answer is "yes," is it because of your difficult ministry context? Or is it you? In other words, are you doing your part to minimize conflicts (practicing the above suggestions), or are you a combative youth minister?

Ask a trusted mentor, coworker, or volunteer to evaluate your conflict style and conflict management effectiveness. This is a very helpful step in becoming a better conflict manager. You may hear things you do not want to hear, but as iron sharpens iron, you will receive tremendous direction for improving your conflict game. Seek evaluation from those who can be objective and not just tell you what you want to hear.

If you are married, have a conversation with your spouse about your conflict style and conflict management. He or she knows you better than anyone else. Listen to your spouse.

"It is time to have a conversation with him!"

I saw my former boss pull out of a restaurant in front of me. That is when I heard the words.

It was not an audible voice, but it might as well have been. The Holy Spirit spoke to me clearly. I had to act.

I followed him to the church building parking lot, pulled up beside him, spoke a few nervous, casual greetings (I really did not want to visit), and then spoke to, not around, the issue. "I have been in ministry for thirty years and have never left a church like I did when I left here," I explained.

What followed was an open, difficult, clarifying, respectful, and affirming conversation that put everything relevant on the table for viewing.

The result? A burden was lifted off our shoulders, a path toward resolution was found, and a relationship was restored.

CONCLUDING TRUTH: CONFLICT MATTERS.

ENTERTAINMENT
MATTERS

"David, do you hear the language in this movie?!"

"No, what is wrong with it?"

"There are all kinds of curse words!"

"Really?"

My wife and I have played this conversation over and over in our twenty-seven-year marriage. The truth is that I don't hear curse words unless they are the "big ones" (words that begin with an "F" and use the Lord's name incorrectly). Not in my home, but I grew up hearing curse words my whole life. I am sad to say my "word radar" is broken.

So apart from the classic *Princess Bride*, *Napoleon Dynamite*, and *Star Wars* movies, I have not hosted many youth group movie outings. I simply do not trust myself to select the right movie.

I do better with video games, but they have their own difficulties.

"I am offended that you are letting the students play *Halo*."

The parent was livid that we would be having a *Halo* tournament at our end-of-year celebration. What followed was a series of conversations on game ratings and how an "M" (mature) rated game can be changed to a "T" (teen) rated game in certain settings.

If you haven't yet, you soon will have tension over entertainment choices in youth ministry. Choose your activities wisely.

TRUTH: ENTERTAINMENT MATTERS.

WHY?

Entertainment is a crucial element in youth ministry programming because it offers an opportunity to create and strengthen relationships.[1] Yes, movies, mud fights, slip and slides, and scavenger hunts have a theological purpose in youth ministry. Entertainment choices must also be made with safety, appropriateness, and righteousness in mind.

Safety. Any youth ministry activity has an element of risk involved. Work to minimize risk, and be prepared for crisis.[2]

Appropriateness. Some entertainment is more appropriate for different age groups, genders, and skill levels. For example, it is appropriate to play two-below touch football with a same-gender group of participants, but you do not play two-below touch football in a mixed-gender group (unless you want to get fired). Or, it is appropriate to take a broad skill-level group of participants on a short hike to enjoy a picnic at camp, but you do not take a broad skill-level group of participants on a climb to summit a fourteen-thousand-foot-high mountain peak. Remember, slow down your excitement over an entertainment idea, and think through appropriateness. A great entertainment idea can quickly become a horrible entertainment idea.

Righteousness. The concert, video game, movie, or other idea may be the newest and most hyped entertainment program of the teen world. Still, as the youth minister, your job is to encourage, model, and instruct in righteous entertainment choices.

> But among you there must not be even a hint of sexual immorality, or of any kind of impurity, or of greed, because these are improper for God's holy people. Nor should there be obscenity, foolish talk or coarse joking, which are out of place, but rather thanksgiving (Eph. 5:3–4).

> Don't let anyone look down on you because you are young, but set an example for the believers in speech, in conduct, in love, in faith and in purity (1 Tim. 4:12).

There are many verses[3] that can be used to support our efforts to choose righteous entertainment options. However, the two above settled the issue for me long ago.

"David, are you kidding me? If these verses represent the standard, there are few entertainment options to choose from in today's youth ministry context!"

Yes, it is very difficult to choose a concert, video game, movie, or other entertainment choice for programming. And yes, most of the families to which you will minister will have a much less strict standard than you. Still, that does not change the expectation you have as a youth minister.

HOW?

Entertainment can be found almost anywhere in youth ministry. Really!

If you have a roll of duct tape and a ball, you can play four square, dodgeball, and indoor "nukem" volleyball. If you have chairs in your youth room, you can play Take a Hike (Fruit Basket Turnover), Bun Shuffle, Wink 'em (if you do not know what that game is, well, it is awesome), or musical chairs. If you have nothing, play the quiet game until everyone is laughing. The point is simple—entertainment can be found anywhere and fit any ministry budget or no budget at all. Below are a few things to remember when programming entertainment for your youth ministry.

Less is more. Especially with high-school-aged students, less is more. Teenagers are busy and need time to just be, without an agenda. For camps and retreats, provide various entertainment options (all the "ball sports," board games, canoeing, art options, hammocking, etc.) that are relaxing and not too competitive. For periodic hang out times, depending on the size of your group, play things that everyone can be involved with, such as ultimate frisbee, hide-and-seek, musical chairs, Take a Hike, and other such games.

More for less. When you have the budget, look for ways to maximize the amount of entertainment you can provide your students. Invite other youth ministries to partner with you in bringing in a band or reserving an amusement park location or some other high-dollar entertainment event. Ask for lower prices. Sometimes parks, entertainers, bands, and other providers will make deals with you. It never hurts to ask.

Transform the old. Do you remember the games you liked to play as a kid? Tag, hide-and-seek, red rover, crab soccer, and I Spy are examples. Or the games you got in trouble for playing? Food fights, mud fights, and spitball fights are examples. All of these can be transformed into modern, memorable, and money-wise entertainment options.

Hype helps. How you pitch an entertainment program is crucial. Seriously! For example, about every other year we have students work in teams to creatively present the Twenty-Third Psalm. They can choose their style—rap, country, rock, classical, musical, or opera are the choices. It has always been entertaining to see their performances. To add hype, we offer prizes for first, second, and third place. These are extravagant prizes gathered from the dollar aisles of a national chain store. Students will work themselves to death to attain a princess crown, superhero cape, silly putty, movie poster, glow-in-the-dark stars, dinosaur play sets, and other fine prizes for their team. It sounds silly, but it works and provides a lot of entertainment. The more you play up the unbelievable value, the more fun everyone will have.

Competitive entertainment. It is great fun and takes relatively little money to host a tournament of some sort. Videogaming, laser tag, Monopoly, basketball, kickball, dodgeball, etc., and all the fantasy sports brackets can be worked into a tournament event. Caution: Be careful to post clear rules and monitor the level of competition. Student and adult volunteers can lose their minds when placed in a competitive situation. My advice is to not have too many competitive entertainment events, as they seem to leave more people hurting than happy.

Non-competitive entertainment. In my opinion, this is the sweet spot of youth ministry. Find entertainment in which all types of talented and abled people can participate on close to the same level. How about an egg-and-spoon relay? A food fight? A greased watermelon shuttle? A water balloon fight? Again, find a way for everyone to feel comfortable and welcomed into the activity.

Know and respect your context. Remember when your mom would say, "Don't throw the ball in the house"? Same concept. Certain entertainment options need to take place outdoors, and some need to occur indoors. You need to know what is permitted in various locations. Do your homework to save yourself from avoidable problems.

Video games. Ratings, ratings, ratings. And, be sure people are comfortable with first-person shooter-type games.

Concerts and entertainers. They are fun, but it can be rather expensive to get the bands and entertainers you want. Remember "more for less," and work together with other youth ministries. Catching a band before they make it big can make them much more affordable. Also, reach out to entertainers and ask if they could come to your venue for a certain price. All they can say is "no," and they often say "yes."

Movies. Ratings, ratings, ratings. But that is not all. Some PG-13 movies are as bad or worse than R-rated films. Be sure to preview before you view with your students.

How much is too much? Keep the main thing the main thing. Remember that entertainment is crucial to youth ministry in that it presents opportunity for the creation and strengthening of relationships. Youth ministry programming should be entertaining, but even so, entertainment without depth is just wrong. You may draw a crowd, but are you drawing them to Jesus? You are responsible for the balance. Play hard, and work hard.

 NOW?

Finding entertainment sources for youth ministry programming is a constant challenge. The above "how" pointers will help you meet that challenge with excellence. What now?

Take and bake. You probably have some programming event coming up in which entertainment is a part. If you already have an entertainment event planned, "bake" it a little longer. Ask yourself: How can I add hype to the event? How can I make it bigger and more memorable? Be creative.

Plan some entertainment. No budget, no problem. Be creative with what you have around you as a resource. Have a budget, and make the most of it. Find ways to maximize the resources you have been given. Be creative, and remember that the goal is the creation and strengthening of relationships. Have fun.

One final word. Unless clearly stated, do not use an entertainment event as an opportunity to share the gospel. This is a bait and switch and does not go over well in today's culture.

"Dude. We just had a snowball fight in August!"

Yes, we had a real snowball fight (not the newspaper kind). I found a shaved ice company that makes snowballs out of their shaved ice and ships them to your location. It was awesome!

I took three hundred-plus students into the heat of Texas and had them stand there until it was unbearably hot. When they'd had enough, I called for a hidden van carrying hundreds of snowballs to drive onto the field. Soon after, the magic happened. A snowball fight, with real snow, in the middle of August!

Relationships were created and strengthened. We made a memory that will last a lifetime.

CONCLUDING TRUTH: ENTERTAINMENT MATTERS.

MARRIAGE
MATTERS

"If this is what youth ministry is going to be like, I am out!"

My wife and I had been married for six months when we began our first youth ministry job. I was twenty-one and she was nineteen. We followed a single, interim youth minister who had done an incredible job getting the ministry ready for transition. He gave us a great gift by setting up the entire summer schedule so that Lisa and I could concentrate on acclimating to our new ministry and building relationships.

In retrospect, both he and I would conclude later that the amount of activity was out of balance, but Lisa and I were young and naive, and we jumped into our new adventure at fullspeed. That summer was like driving a racing go-cart on a rain-soaked slick track. You have your foot on the floor, arrogantly controlling the slippage on the corners with your "professional" driving skills, until "bam!" A car sharing the track taps you on the turn. You find yourself in an uncontrollable spin, coming to a sudden stop, facing the oncoming cars, waiting for someone to complete your humiliation by running across the track to correct your direction and get you back in the race.

Get the picture? That was how my first summer in youth ministry concluded.

"I am done with youth ministry!" said the other driver on the track, my wife of six months.

Very quickly, we realized the pace at which we were racing was unsustainable and destructive to our marriage. We were fortunate that those running across the track to correct our direction were church leaders who cared deeply about the success of our marriage. They did much more than teach us how to tap the brakes on slick turns. They pulled us out of the car and off the slick track. Our leaders demanded we slow down, go to a class with our peers,[1] and make use of our youth team (parents) to better organize the ministry.

"We are fine!" was how I arrogantly responded when my leaders first approached. I am so thankful these godly men and women looked past my arrogance, pride, and insecurity to lovingly demand I take care of my marriage first. Their lessons continue to echo in our minds, lessons that have sustained our youth ministry marriage for more than twenty-six years.

TRUTH: MARRIAGE MATTERS.

WHY?

Marriage is intended to be a reflection of the intimate love, devotion, and sacrifice Christ has for his church. Therefore, a youth minister's marriage is one of the greatest, if not the greatest, testimonies and tools he has to impact the lives of teenagers with the gospel of Jesus.

> That is why a man leaves his father and mother and
> is united to his wife, and they become one flesh
> (Gen. 2:24).

Submit to one another out of reverence for Christ
(Eph. 5:21).

"For this reason a man will leave his father and
mother and be united to his wife, and the two will
become one flesh." This is a profound mystery—but
I am talking about Christ and the church. However,
each one of you also must love his wife as he loves
himself, and the wife must respect her husband
(Eph. 5:31–33).

Wives, submit yourselves to your husbands, as is
fitting in the Lord. Husbands, love your wives and do
not be harsh with them (Col. 3:18–19).

. . . so that no one will malign the word of God
(Titus 2:5b).

. . . so that those who oppose you may be ashamed
because they have nothing bad to say about us
(Titus 2:8b).

Early on in our ministry, I was not affectionate with my wife in
public. Really. I did not hold her hand, kiss her goodbye, put
my arm around her at the camp dinner table, or cuddle with her
by the campfire. Don't get me wrong—I loved doing all those
things in private, but for some reason, I did not think it appropriate to do this in front of teenagers. That is when my wife, a
product of a single-parent upbringing due to divorce, taught
me how important the testimony and witness of a healthy marriage can be in a teenager's life.

"David, we may be the only healthy marriage a student
sees," she said. "They need to know what a healthy, affectionate, devoted, sacrificial relationship looks like."

That conversation ended my avoidance of public displays of affection (PDA). Even though students, including our own, love yelling "that's gross," we continue to think of our marriage as a testimony and tool of the gospel. More than once, a student from long ago has posted on social media or communicated in a private message his or her gratitude for how we lived our marriage in front of them. Students also witnessed moments when our marriage was not so affectionate because we were not having a "good day." That's real life. While being authentic, we are appropriate with our public relationship. We understand, and so do our teenagers, that a great marriage has a level of intimacy that is protected and shared with each other and God alone.

Because of the tremendous power a healthy marriage has to validate and spread the gospel of Jesus, I believe Satan has targeted marriages. Think about it. How many students and families would be shaken if your marriage failed? Take care of your marriage.

HOW?

Choice is inherent in relationship. A great marriage is based on making great choices. A choice to follow Jesus as Lord is foundational (read all those verses again). You build upon that foundation by making a choice to sacrificially love your spouse. It is easy to understand but difficult to execute. That is why I am writing about choice instead of feeling. Feelings are easily manipulated. A choice is something you can make when you don't feel like making it.

Make the choice to leave and cleave. This is one of the greatest and most recognizable marriage verses in the Bible.

The man said, "This is now bone of my bones and
flesh of my flesh; she shall be called 'woman,' for she
was taken out of man." That is why a man leaves his
father and mother and is united to his wife, and they
become one flesh (Gen. 2:23–24).

Yes, "one flesh" is a term that gets middle school students gig-
gling, but the term involves much more than the sexual union
between a husband and wife. The term is referring to a level
of intimacy marriages can reach only through making a daily
choice to pursue a lifestyle of sacrificial love. A choice to leave
one's family and cleave to one's spouse takes a lot of sacrificial
love from both husband and wife.

It is imperative that the "leave and cleave" of marriage is
in a state of constant growth to survive the challenges of youth
ministry, or any ministry, for that matter. How is your leave-
and-cleave strength?

* When faced with a challenge, do you turn to your
  spouse first, or to a parent or friend?
* Whose opinion weighs more on how you make decisions in your marriage? Your spouse? A parent?
  A friend?
* When having a bad day, who do you call first? Your
  spouse? A parent? A friend?

The answers to these questions can help reveal the level of leave-
and-cleave in your marriage. If your answers indicated a low
level of leaving and cleaving, make the sacrificial and loving
choice to pursue a "one flesh" marriage.

Make the choice to communicate. Youth ministers are communicators. You will do almost anything to get and hold the

attention of teenagers so a message can be delivered. Do you make the same determined choice to communicate with your spouse? Communication is vital to a marriage—it's the water that allows growth, and it's the gasoline that allows the engine to fire and the wheels to turn. And, you need to intentionally do it well.

* Choose to listen more than you speak.
* Choose to speak your needs clearly.
* Choose to lower the intensity of your tone.
* Choose to speak kind words.
* Choose to keep confidence with and in your spouse.
* Choose to look into the eyes when you speak.
* Choose to give undivided attention.
* Choose to engage in topics your spouse cares about.
* Choose to withdraw from a conversation when things get too heated.
* Choose to rejoin the conversation so that understanding occurs.
* Again, choose to listen.

Especially in times of conflict, which happen from time to time in a marriage, the following verse is right on point:

> My dear brothers and sisters, take note of this:
> Everyone should be quick to listen, slow to speak
> and slow to become angry, because human anger
> does not produce the righteousness that God desires.
> Therefore, get rid of all moral filth and the evil that is
> so prevalent and humbly accept the word planted in
> you, which can save you (James 1:19–21).

I did not say it was an easy verse to hear, but some choices are difficult to make. Communication may be one of those choices.

Make the choice to protect and strengthen intimacy. The word "intimacy" evokes a sexual context. Yet, like the term "one flesh," it is a holistic word that encompasses the quality of the entire marriage relationship. To be fully known and fully accepted in a relationship is an intimate goal that involves emotional, spiritual, and physical closeness. It also requires a choice to sacrificially love.

What kinds of choices protect intimacy?

* A choice to maintain great communication
* A choice to make time with your spouse a priority
* A choice to let go and move away from past failures
* A choice to respect and support your spouse
* A choice to stay away from and guard against pornography (visual and emotional)
* A choice to connect with your spouse on a sexual level
* A choice to connect with your spouse on more than a sexual level

What kinds of choices strengthen intimacy?

* A choice to spend uninterrupted time with your spouse
* A choice to maintain your physical and emotional health
* A choice to pay attention to your spouse in public and private settings
* A choice to use kind and affirming words in communication

* A choice to give nonsexual touch and attention to your spouse
* And yes, a choice to give sexual touch and attention to your spouse

You may have noticed a few of those statements seem to contradict themselves. Actually, they do not. They work together and should exist in balance. Touch needs to mean more than a precursor to sex in a marriage, and touch also needs to be playful and a precursor to sex in a marriage. A deep intimacy will help a spouse know when and what type of touch is needed. Do you want more sexual intimacy in your marriage? There is a simple word that is helpful to remember in protecting and strengthening sexual intimacy in your marriage: "increase." Increased intimacy leads to increased desire, which leads to an increase in sexual intimacy.

Make the choice to control the burn of youth ministry. Stay off the slick track if you want to travel the long-haul road of youth ministry. There are seasons in the youth ministry calendar that are just busier than others, and realizing and preparing for the busy seasons is key to controlling the burn of youth ministry. Lisa and I have visited with countless couples in our twenty-six years of marriage and youth ministry. Couples who do not acknowledge, fail to prepare for, and constantly complain about these youth ministry "seasons" often experience a high level of stress in their marriages.

The time commitment of youth ministry is often unpredictable and fluid. Still, a youth minister can make choices that regulate the burn.

* Make the choice to talk to your spouse about upcoming seasons of youth ministry.

* Make the choice to put your family calendar before the youth ministry calendar.
* Make the choice to give your spouse veto power of the proposed youth calendar before presenting to leadership and parents.
* Make the choice to work hard so you can rest and play hard.
* Make the choice to give your first fruits of energy and attention to your spouse.
* Make the choice to take your day off.
* Make the choice to protect time to date your spouse.
* Make the choice to take your vacation days.
* Make the choice to limit back-to-back trips and weekend activities.
* Make the choice to turn off your phone and limit the time you spend on social media platforms.
* Make the choice to be totally present each day with your spouse.

Yes, emergencies happen and you can be called out of your rest into ministry in a moment's notice. Those are manageable and typically understandable by a spouse and family. But if you have a "they need me" Jesus complex and say yes to every request of your time and energy, remember what my youth minister, Phillip Nichols, told me, "There has been only one Savior of the world, there will never be another, and you are not him!" Take a break. Your spouse will thank you!

Make the choice to accept and ask for help. A few of you may have been a little frustrated, or even outright angry, at the beginning of this chapter. You read how my church leaders intervened and helped my marriage survive the early years and thought,

"My leaders care more about results than they do about my struggle to balance my marriage and ministry." I hope that is not the case, but I know many of you are in that type of environment. Even so, your marriage is your responsibility. You may not receive an offer like Lisa and I did, but you can ask for help.

* Make a choice to ask an older ministry couple, inside or outside your church context, for some mentoring time.
* Make a choice to ask a church leader, inside or outside your church context, for some mentoring time.
* Make a choice to reach out to a counselor for a "couple checkup."
* Make the choice to go to a marriage training or conference, and spend time concentrating on your marriage.

If you don't feel comfortable or safe reaching out for help inside your own church context, then go outside that context. Make the choice to ask for and accept help.

 ## NOW?

I am convinced that youth ministers want vibrant marriages.

Reflect. Go back over the "How?" section material with your spouse. Pray together. Practice your communication skills of listening intently and speaking clearly. As you go through each section, ask these questions:

* What is going well?
* What needs improvement?

Again, listen intently and speak clearly. If the conversation becomes confrontational, take a break, or consider having the conversation with a mentoring couple.

Renew. In a context that is focused and private, renew your commitment to do whatever it takes to have an amazing marriage. Sure, a weekend trip to the beach or mountains would be great, but trust me, a focused and private conversation will do wonders for your marriage.

If you ask my wife, "What is your favorite, most memorable moment in your twenty-six-year marriage with David?" she will tell you the story of a swimming pool in Albuquerque, New Mexico. We were staying in Albuquerque on our way to a speaking engagement in northern New Mexico when the weight of a recent miscarriage came crashing down. No words were spoken or needed.

I held her.

We floated.

She quietly shed tears on my chest.

She felt safe and secure knowing that she was my one and only focused concern.

Of course, we have had other not-so-fabulous moments in our marriage, moments in which we fought for our right and our way. Yet, we continue to make the choice to pursue a great marriage.

CONCLUDING TRUTH: MARRIAGE MATTERS.

MISSION TRIPS AND SERVICE PROJECTS **MATTER**

"In American churches, we fight over the color of carpet, but last week I saw an old lady sweep the dirt floor of her church so that it looked good! We need to get our priorities right!"

One of our senior students said this during a Sunday night summer report worship program. Actually, we had just finished a building renovation, so the deafening silence in the auditorium was very noticeable. This senior had been changed by his experience on a short-term mission trip, a trip he had participated in during several years. This time something clicked—life for this young man would forever be different.

"I am moving to New York!"

The young man who spoke these words, a new believer, had just completed a short-term mission trip to New York City. During the trip and continuing for weeks after, he felt a tug by the Holy Spirit to change his "predictable" go-to-college-after-high-school trajectory. So he moved to New York and worked with a local church for a year. And yes, he eventually went to college and completed his studies. He grew from that life-changing experience.

"Can I sell candy in the youth center?"

The young lady had been touched by a message delivered by an organization that works to end sex trafficking in the United States and around the world. She had heard in the message that a few hundred dollars enables this organization to deliver a young lady out of the sex trafficking industry. She took the challenge to heart and developed a plan to sell candy in order to raise money for this cause. She raised over $1,500! The message had changed and challenged the status quo in this young lady's heart. She had only one option of response: serve.

TRUTH: MISSION TRIPS AND SERVICE PROJECTS MATTER.

WHY?

Christians have a standing order to follow. A standing order is to be followed regardless of changing circumstances. Whether your youth group is small or large, a standing order must be followed. Whether your youth group is well-resourced or under-resourced, a standing order must be followed. Whether your youth group meets in a prime spot or terrible location, a standing order must be followed.

> Then Jesus came to them and said, "All authority in heaven and on earth has been given to me. Therefore go and make disciples of all nations, baptizing them in the name of the Father and of the Son and of the Holy Spirit, and teaching them to obey everything I have commanded you. And surely I am with you always, to the very end of the age" (Matt. 28:18–20).

We call it the Great Commission, and it needs to be taken seriously by every follower of Jesus. I am not going to parse out every nuance of this passage. From a surface read, the message is clear: go and make disciples. Whether local, domestic, or foreign, Christians are on a mission.

Christians have an example of service to follow. In one of his most unforgettable "active learning" lessons, Jesus set the standard for service.

> When he had finished washing their feet, he put
> on his clothes and returned to his place. "Do you
> understand what I have done for you?" he asked
> them. "You call me 'Teacher' and 'Lord,' and rightly
> so, for that is what I am. Now that I, your Lord and
> Teacher, have washed your feet, you also should wash
> one another's feet. I have set you an example that you
> should do as I have done for you. Very truly I tell
> you, no servant is greater than his master, nor is a
> messenger greater than the one who sent him. Now
> that you know these things, you will be blessed if you
> do them" (John 13:12–17).

Many of us have washed each other's feet, yet the message here is meant for much more than an activity suggestion. We are to do as Jesus did: serve.

If we want to justify who gets to receive such extravagant service, Jesus gave us the teaching of the Good Samaritan.

> "Which of these three do you think was a neighbor
> to the man who fell into the hands of robbers?" The
> expert in the law replied, "The one who had mercy
> on him."

Jesus told him, "Go and do likewise" (Luke 10:36–37).

Missions and service activities go hand in hand and should be a central component of any youth ministry programming.

Jesus gave the order and set the example. "Go and do likewise," indeed.

HOW?

Youth ministers want their students to develop a lifestyle of service and mission. Youth ministers provide short-term mission and service opportunities in order to teach and inspire that lifestyle choice in students.

Asking the right questions. Mission and service are essential, but it's important to ask the right questions during your program planning.

Will this activity hurt or help those we are serving? Of course, it will be helpful, you say. But are you sure? Slow down and really answer the question. For example, many U.S. youth ministries go into third world countries and/or devastated areas and rebuild homes, churches, schools, and other types of infrastructure. At face value, there is nothing wrong with such activity, which seems rather noble to spend time doing. However, what if the local economy is counting on local residents working on and supplying such rebuilding efforts? You may have just taken jobs away from those needing the work to support their families. Another example: youth ministries love to serve and/or give clothes to those on the streets. Again, at face value, what can be wrong with such service? In some situations, those receiving the help will use your gift as leverage to get something out of their fellow homeless citizens.

How do you determine what is hurtful or helpful? The simplest way is to ask questions and listen. Ask:

* City, state, and national government agencies
* The church, school, or agency you are wanting to serve
* Local, domestic, or international mission or service organizations
* Your church's mission or service leadership teams
* The people you would like to serve

Ask them:

* "How can we serve you, your mission, your people?
* "If my youth group came and did _____, would that help or hurt you, your organization, or your culture?"

And listen to their responses.

Does this activity align with our church's mission and service activities? If you ask the right questions, you will know this answer quickly. No, not every short-term mission or service opportunity will perfectly align with that of your church. Still, strive for alignment, which gives your students an opportunity to feel like a part of your church's overall mission and enables them to work alongside adult church members. That connection is vital if you want your students to really comprehend what a lifestyle of service and mission looks like.

Is the cost for participation in this activity reasonable and accessible to students? Mission trips, especially international short-term projects, can be expensive. Work to make travel and lodging as cheap as possible. If you have an adult volunteer who is a travel agent or involved in a related field of work, tap them for assistance. The more reasonable the price, the more accessible the trip will be for broad student participation. In other words, if possible, be sure that all students, including those both with and without financial resources, can participate.

Is this mission or service activity sustainable? There are two parts to this question. One, is it possible to develop a long-term partnership and strategy with the target of your mission or service? Especially in connection with local service opportunities, it is best to think long-term rather than short-term. For example, thinking back to "hurtful" or "helpful," showing up to a nursing home once a year can be detrimental to a senior citizen by highlighting loneliness. However, committing to monthly visits helps students and residents build meaningful connections that combat loneliness. Two, is the work you are doing able to be carried on by others when you leave? Is it sustainable? For example, when helping a church with a Vacation Bible School outreach, others should be able to follow up with the children and families that attend after your youth group leaves.

How will you know you have been successful in your mission or service? This is an important question. With physical missions and service opportunities (construction, medical care, yard work, demolition, cleanup, etc.), it is rather easy to determine whether your efforts were a success or failure. Relational missions and service opportunities (VBS, camp ministry, outreach conferences/meetings, etc.) are more difficult to evaluate as successes or failures. Other than numbers of participants and the occasional story of conversions, the fruit of relational missions and service is often slow to develop. Regardless, it is important to let your students know what success will look like if their mission and service opportunity is carried out with excellence. Your church leadership will also more than likely want to hear a report of the impact your short-term mission or service opportunity had on your target audience. Be prepared with numbers, pictures, and stories from the field.

These questions are not the end-all, but they provide a solid starting spot for your mission and service programming.

Other considerations. Here are a few more items you will want to keep in mind while conducting mission and service programming:

Process. Process. Process! Before, during, and after the mission or service activity, talk to your students and volunteers about the importance of what they are doing and why they are doing it. Ask them to share their experiences, challenges, and victories. In other words, make the time you spend on mission and service as practical and contextual as possible. Without process, students will be tempted to see service as if it was just another thing to do instead of the main thing Christians do with their lives.

Training. I realize you cannot provide training before every service opportunity. Even so, take the time before major trips or service opportunities to educate your students on the why's of mission and service (you can use the information in the section above as a starting place), and give them an understanding of the culture and context in which they will be serving. Note: The days of participating in a certain number of service projects to qualify for a mission trip is outdated. Students are busy. Change your training accountability standard and use the time you take to train.

Education. Never stop learning. I highly recommend *Deep Justice in a Broken World* by Chap Clark and Kara Powell and *Sticky Faith Service Guide* by Kara Powell and Brad Griffin as resources for starting your educational journey. They will give you and your team many more strategic questions to ask before launching a short-term mission or service effort with your student ministry. They will also offer training ideas and several processing tips for your students and volunteers.

Closing thoughts. I have two. First, many of your students may come to you for service hours. These hours may be part of a school class expectation, or they may be working off a traffic ticket. Regardless, do not make them feel bad for their request, but also don't relax the high expectations you have for mission and service work. It can be an interesting balancing act, so be careful. Second, many short-term mission trips plan a fun day to celebrate the completed work week. These entertainment times are wonderful for building and strengthening relationships. However, do not let fun day expectations eclipse work responsibilities.

 NOW?

Mission and service activity is not just what we do, it is who we are as followers of Christ. It is our standing order. It is what we see Jesus doing, and we go and do likewise.

Change your language. The first thing you can do to show that mission trips and service opportunities matter is to change your language. Speak of every day as an opportunity to be on mission and serve others. Speak of that upcoming mission trip or service activity as an opportunity to be Jesus to the world. Change your speech.

Raise your expectations. I am pretty strong about this one. Yes, relationships are built and strengthened by participation in short-term mission trips and service opportunities. Still, that is not the main reason youth ministers program such activity. Mission and service (broken record here) are our standing order and "go and do likewise" example. Therefore, the goal for student participation is not to become part of the youth group. Rather, the goal for student participation is to learn how to join Jesus in his work. Everything else is serendipitous.

"Our brothers from Mexico have driven all night to spend time with our church family."

Our church family had just experienced the worst tragedy in our history.[1] Hearing of the event, the church family we had been working with for close to five years made the difficult trip across the border and into the fellowship hall of our church building.

Humbled and honored by their presence, we were comforted by hugs, words shared through broken English and butchered Spanish, and tears that ran down our faces like a river.

We had partnered with them in ministry on their side of the border. They came to our side and partnered with us as we struggled to pick up the pieces.

To this day, that moment is held deeply in my heart with great appreciation. That moment represents a countable success. A sustainable, well-thought-out, aligned, and helpful short-term mission was producing the fruit.

CONCLUDING TRUTH: MISSION TRIPS AND SERVICE PROJECTS MATTER.

OFFICE HOURS
MATTER

"You know youth ministers; he is out doing something."

This was how my secretary informed the anxious parent about my unknown whereabouts. Needless to say, I was not happy with the way the situation was handled, especially since I had told her where I would be and what I would be doing (she forgot). The response given was silly, and I did not like it. It was unprofessional and had the potential of ruining my credibility with that family.

That statement had come from somewhere. After digging a bit, I found out that many of the youth ministers this person had worked with previously had little regard for office hours, kept odd hours, or rarely let the office know where they were during work hours. This left the secretary in an uncomfortable situation when she received those "Is the youth minister in the office?" phone calls, and she often did not know how to answer that question.

When we understood where each of us was coming from, an even more effective system of office hours accountability was developed that made both of us happy.

She was informed, and I was accurately represented.

She knew where I was and could reach me if necessary.

She knew that my work took me out of the office, and I appreciated the backup when someone questioned my absence.

Why was this such a big deal to settle?

TRUTH: OFFICE HOURS MATTER.

WHY?

The youth minister's job description often takes him or her out of the office and into the places where teenagers dwell. This can lead to erratic office hours. However, many parents and church leaders do not understand or know how to quantify such hours. As the youth minister, it is your responsibility to clearly communicate your availability and location to those who need to know, like your secretary or administrative assistant. These all have a context, but the concepts of dependability and responsibility are the scene in these scriptures:

> All you need to say is simply "Yes" or "No"; anything beyond this comes from the evil one (Matt. 5:37).

> Do your best to present yourself to God as one approved, a worker who does not need to be ashamed and who correctly handles the word of truth (2 Tim. 2:15).

> But you, keep your head in all situations, endure hardship, do the work of an evangelist, discharge all the duties of your ministry (2 Tim. 4:5).

> One who is slack in his work is brother to one who destroys (Prov. 18:9).

Youth ministers are allies and a trusted presence in the spiritual development of teenagers. Your dependable and responsible presence (inside and outside the office) strengthens that trust with parents, adult volunteers, church leaders, and teenagers.

If you say you are going to be in the office, then be in the office.

If you feel you need more assistance with programming, then be in the office.

If you feel you need more time to pour into your lessons, then be in the office.

If you feel you need more uninterrupted time in your office, then communicate that need.

I realize some of you are thinking, "I get my best study done away from my office." If so, communicate where you will be and how long so that you can be available in the office. For your youth ministry to run smoothly, you need to have a regular presence in the office.

HOW?

Office hours need not be a burden. In fact, they can assist you in doing your job as a youth minister. Make the most of the time you have been given. Here are some helpful tips.

Get to the office on time. If you are supposed to be at the office by 8:00 A.M., then be there at 7:59 A.M. The credibility from such conduct will pay off when you need to take that extra time to recoup from an exhausting trip. Regarding Mondays after a weekend trip, most of the jobs your parents and adult volunteers work at expect that office hours be kept with excellence and accountability. Regardless of whether they sponsored a weekend youth retreat, they will be at work, on time, the next day. I expect the same type of office hours out of my employees. If it is not a day off, then get to work, on time.

Do meaningful work. Yes, there will be times when you will have, or feel like you have, nothing to accomplish in the office. At such times, take time to read, catch up on emails, plan ahead, or listen to that podcast. Most of the time, you will have an upcoming event and/or lesson to work on. The key is organizing and prioritizing your time in the office.

Work out a system of accountability. If you leave the office, let your secretary or administrative assistant know where you are going and when you hope to return. There are multiple levels of helpful accountability here, so be thankful for the system. If you do not have secretarial or administrative help, tell a staff member. Be accountable.

Pay attention to your dress and to the condition of your office space. Your office will more than likely have a dress code—abide by that code. And remember, like a doctor's office, your office space reflects the perception of your ability to care for those who will be sitting with you in that space. Keep things clean and organized.

Keep your door open or have a window in your door. It is imperative that you keep your actions in your office viewable to others. It is never appropriate to meet with someone behind closed, non-windowed doors. Such behavior invites vulnerability to accusation.

Don't be "that person." Don't whine about how hard your job is. Youth ministry hours can be different, but don't make the mistake of thinking this means you work harder than any other person on staff. That is not a true statement. All ministry is difficult and often happens after "office hours."

Keeping regular office hours can reduce a youth minister's preparation stress and create space for deep reflection, personal growth, and programming.

NOW?

Make the choice to make the most out of your time in the office. Youth ministers can strengthen or change the way they use office hours by starting with one practical choice.

Ask yourself a question. If a student or parent came into your office, would they feel you have a professional and welcoming space? If not, straighten up that office, my friend.

Pick a "how" suggestion and get to work. Are each of the "how" suggestions a part of your office hours practice? If not, change your practice(s). You may want to start by assuring you show up on time tomorrow morning.

"Here's what is coming your way, David."

My administrative assistant knew from the tone of the phone call that the family was not happy, and the unavoidable meeting that was about to take place could be difficult to navigate.

Thankfully, our office hours practice and teamwork gave us an idea of how to handle such an occasion.

I was able to give time, attention, safety, and answers to the family's concern. We were prepared, and it led to an opportunity for ministry to happen.

CONCLUDING TRUTH: OFFICE HOURS MATTER.

ORGANIZATION
MATTERS

"I am sorry, but I lost over a thousand dollars in cash and checks."

I spoke these words to my finance director after a weekend retreat. I searched everywhere and could not find the bag that contained all the money and checks from our just-completed retreat registration (youth ministers carried money bags around before there was more convenient technology available). I concluded that I must have left the money bag in the side door of the van and that someone must have broken into the van and taken the money. Since I always thought of myself as a fairly organized person, this was an embarrassing admission.

Months later, I was cleaning up my office and went through a satchel (the satchel was another tool youth ministers carried before smartphones and laptops). Inside, I found the lost money bag.

If you think telling your finance director about the loss is embarrassing, try telling him you found the money and now-voided checks. The robbery scenario was a much more exciting story to tell than my simply losing the money by throwing a satchel into an office cabinet. In short, I lost the money because I was disorganized.

From that point forward, I stepped up and improved the organization of my office, activities, time, and resources.

TRUTH: ORGANIZATION MATTERS.

 WHY?

Youth ministers feel the burden of responsibility for the execution of their ministry and the well-being of the students in their care. An organized youth minister gives parents and guardians more peace and confidence when releasing their student into the youth minister's care. Conversely, an unorganized youth minister raises alarm.

> Sluggards do not plow in season; so at harvest time they look but find nothing (Prov. 20:4).

> Put your outdoor work in order and get your fields ready; after that, build your house (Prov. 24:27).

> There is a time for everything, and a season for every activity under the heavens (Eccles. 3:1).

> For there is a proper time and procedure for every matter, though a person may be weighed down by misery (Eccles. 8:6).

Organization of time, energy, and resources (mental and physical) are implied in all these verses. You need to carry out your duties with as much excellence as you can muster. That takes organization!

You do not need to be so organized that a misplaced file or a schedule pushed back by fifteen minutes sends you into a frenzy. Youth ministry is often synonymous with interruption. As you read the Gospels, much of Jesus's ministry was a series of interruptions. Control your own time and manage these interruptions—don't let the interruptions manage you. This is what Jesus did.

> Therefore Jesus no longer moved about publicly among the people of Judea. Instead he withdrew to a region near the wilderness, to a village called Ephraim, where he stayed with his disciples (John 11:54).

> As the time approached for him to be taken up to heaven, Jesus resolutely set out for Jerusalem (Luke 9:51).

An organized youth minister is more productive and radiates a confidence that gives both students and adults comfort.

HOW?

Youth ministers did not answer the call to ministry because they are gifted in accounting, organizational management, or event planning. Still, that is not an excuse to avoid learning and developing organization skills. Organization is important.

The following are a number of practices I have strengthened and developed since I solved the case of the missing money bag.

Plan ahead. This may seem obvious, but if you do not plan for planning, it will not happen. Especially in today's culture when family calendars fill up fast, there is little patience for an activity that is thrown together at the last minute or feels like it has been. There are three seasons in a youth minister's year: winter-spring (January–May), summer (June–August), and fall

(September–December).[1] Planning happens in these various "seasons" of the youth ministry year.[2]

Year. Some programming is planned at least a year in advance. A standing camp, retreat, or mission trip, an out-of-country program, or a standing church weekend assembly or conference are examples of year-ahead planned activities. Not that all the details are finalized, but the date should be secured within a range of at least a few days. It's also a great idea to schedule your planning meetings a year in advance (at least know the month these events will occur). Each church and corresponding youth ministry, large or small, typically has its own month in which the yearly calendar items are expected to be coordinated. This often corresponds to budget formation. For budgeting purposes, you don't have to have all the details planned, but you need a solid understanding of all the programming you will be executing so you can budget accordingly.

Six months. Curriculum, special events (concerts, movie nights, trampoline park outings, game days, etc.), worship nights, small group nights, parent meetings, and preparation meetings are all examples of six-months-out planning. In my experience, it works well to have two intensive planning meetings each year in your student ministry: a meeting in August that covers the fall season and a meeting in November that covers winter-spring, summer, and the entire year. This is just a suggestion—each youth minister will know what month works best in his context. With that said, a word of warning: if you wait until May to plan and communicate the summer schedule of programming, you will be beaten down with backlash from parents and students. All families—suburban, city, and rural— need at least a six-month cushion to plan their calendars. Remember, our families and students are busy.

Month. If your year and six-month calendar have been organized, your month is organized to execute the plan. In other words, your monthly organization is determined by the details involved in conducting each program. Monthly organization provides a macroview of the upcoming workload a youth minister can expect in the coming weeks.

Week. The week is organized so that the youth minister can complete program execution. Weekly organization is a microview that provides the greatest source of to-do items that helps the youth minister manage and balance his work schedule. The youth minister's week is filled with work that impacts a program that is happening in that week or is going to happen in three weeks. For example, you will, or should, take time to study for a lesson you will be giving that week. You may also be making a shopping run to gather supplies for an upcoming retreat. One of the blessings of youth ministry is that each week is uniquely different.

Get assistance. Surrounding yourself and partnering with good and talented people, people who are better than you in certain areas, is a great leadership practice. Even in smaller youth groups, you are not a self-sustained island. We all need help. My first youth ministry job was tremendous because it taught me the need and blessing of using others to assist in the ministry. It has been my experience that all youth ministries have at least a few individuals that are gifted in organization—they just need to be asked to help. Do you need help with budgeting, file organization, trip planning, registration, food preparation, technology, or leadership development? Look around you.

There may be someone in your church who is a gold mine of talent and is just waiting to be asked to serve.[3]

Get your spaces organized. Have you ever walked into your office or youth ministry closet and had no idea where to find something? Well, and I say this kindly, it's time to get organized! An unorganized space often leads to wasteful use of time. You can't find things (like money bags) or end up creating more documents because you lost the originals in a pile somewhere. The following are a few suggestions for organizing the most common youth ministry spaces.

Office space. Like the office of a medical doctor, your office should be inviting and evoke trust. Yes, youth ministers have the coolest offices (maybe children's ministry is a close competitor), but remember, your office space is a reflection of you and your ministry.

* Files. There is no end to the type of filing systems you could develop. You may opt to keep all your files on your computer or hard drive, but in this case, be sure to back them up. There will also always be a need to keep and file real paper documents and information. You can file alphabetically, by category, and by special grouping. No matter your method, being able to recall a file for reference, reproduction, or refinement is a great asset to your ministry organization.
* Piles. If you have been in ministry for any length of time, you may have begun to notice the desk phenomenon of the pile. Piles are made up of a loose collection of mail, old lessons, ideas written on napkins, notes, cards, sermon notes, books, journals, and pictures drawn by your kids. Organize your piles into

categories. I typically have three piles in my office
space: urgent (I have to get to this within the week),
important (to be used within the next few months),
and go-through (things that I have collected that need
to be filed away or thrown away).

* Cabinets and boxes. I do not know the dimensions of
your particular space. Regardless, make use of your
cabinets and boxes to organize. Paper, envelopes, pens,
staplers, tape (duct tape, of course), and other ministry resources can be tucked away and easily accessible.
Some of the larger piles (like the go-through pile) can
be tucked away in a box or cabinet until needed. Do
not give in to your inner elementary school kid and
stuff all your belongings in a box or cabinet so you can
say you "cleaned your room." Even with things that are
less visible, be organized.

Closets and youth spaces. Clean, organize, and throw away items
in these spaces.

* Clean. Like your office, closets and youth spaces are
a reflection of your ministry. It has been a tradition
in each of my youth ministries to have a cleaning day,
typically more than one, for closets and youth spaces.
* Organize. Shelving and plastic tubs are your
friends. Keep your youth spaces organized for flow
and function.
* Throw away. Confession: I have a tendency to keep
things in closets and youth spaces. I believe it was
when a mouse ran out of the free couch I put in the
youth room that I was done with that tendency. It may

be difficult, but throw away stuff you don't use or have not used in a while, or stuff that is broken.

Organizing information. Youth ministers have lots of information to process and organize (especially when social media use by teenagers and parents is involved). It is imperative that a youth minister, or any leader, for that matter, process and organize information efficiently so they can communicate to their followers proactively, with clarity and vision. Here are a few tips that can help organize and process the flood of information coming into your world:

Handling social media. This source of information, a must for youth ministers to gather, comes at us twenty-four hours a day and has the potential to capture much of our productive time. A few simple tricks: turn off notifications (you decide when you are online); limit the time you are online (it is easy to fall into the habit of habitually checking your status); resist the urge to post everything you read, think, or experience (when you post, you also spend too much time responding); and as much as possible, direct social media "business" messages to your email (this reduces the places you gather and organize information into one).

Handling emails and texts. Unless you are intentional about not doing so, you will probably keep both of these information avenues open during the work day. Again, when appropriate, turn off notifications. With emails, choose specific times of your day when you will open and respond to your correspondence. Use the filing system in your email program (this keeps the inbox clear). If not careful, it is possible to have your day consumed by emails and texts so that no items on your daily to-do list are completed. The world will not end if you do not look at your emails after business hours—they will all still be waiting in your inbox in the morning.

Information reduction. Three phrases to remember are throw away, delete, and file. Frequently go through your piles and files (paper and electronic), and throw away the clutter items you have not used or never will use. Go through your phone voicemails, notes, text messages, and emails, and delete items that are no longer needed. As you go through the reduction process, file, via paper or electronically, information that you feel warrants keeping.

Information download. These strategies work well when you feel overwhelmed by all that needs to be done, when you're working on a big project, or when you just don't know where to start. First, gather all your physical and electronic lists, reminders, notes, and any other to-do sources, and write them all down on one piece of paper. The key is to physically write down the information. After you have exhausted all that you have to do and all that is on your mind, trust me, you will begin to see categories in which the information can be managed and arranged for work. The same type of process can be used for big projects (curriculum, mission trip, camp, retreat) by using a whiteboard. Again, write all the ideas you have for the project on the whiteboard. Be creative and use various colors, pictures, diagrams, and arrows to work and rework the project until you have a workable beginning. Then walk away for a bit (if you cannot guarantee the information will not be erased, take a picture of the board). When you are ready with fresh eyes and mind, go back to the board and rework the project until you have a more refined product. At some point, you will feel like the product on the board is ready to be committed to paper.

Organize your time. If followed, all of the previous strategies will lead to a better organization of your time. With that said, as one youth minister recently confessed, "I am organized, I just don't stick to my plan." Why does this happen? Here are four reasons:

Chronic tardiness. If you are always late, fix it!

The tyranny of the urgent. There is always something that can grab your attention in student ministry, especially if you do not silence various electronic notifications. Every one of these interruptions will feel urgent, but not every one will be critical or a priority at the moment. Only you can determine value, but don't let the urgent captivate your time.

We don't enjoy the work. If there is something in youth ministry that you do not find joy in doing, know that it still needs to be done, and done well, to effectively run a youth ministry.

We didn't say "no." You cannot do everything. Learn to say "no" to things you really want to do but just can't fit into your already busy schedule.

Yes, this was a long section, but organization is crucial if you want to last in youth ministry.

 NOW?

Any organization project, especially if you are inclined toward disorder, can appear overwhelming. As a matter of fact, a few of you may have a disorganized desk, closet, calendar, or pile of receipts that gives you the cold sweats when you consider organizing them. What do you do now to push toward a more organized youth ministry?

Start. Clean your desk, go through that pile of stuff, clean that closet—start somewhere. I recommend you begin with your desk and calendar so that your days will be more organized.

Enlist help. Does a closet or youth space need to be cleaned up? Get some students to help. Does your budget need organization? Get with your church finance director or ask for assistance from a trusted volunteer. Do you need help organizing your youth ministry programming? Go visit with a youth minister peer or reach out to a trusted youth ministry professor or coach.[4]

Be here now. Once you start, you may feel overwhelmed with all there is to organize. If you start feeling that pressure, practice the simple psychological principle of "be here now." That is, be fully present in the moment you are currently occupying. Does this principle sound familiar? Jesus had a lot to say about living in the moment.

Repeat. The process of organizing your ministry is ongoing. Changes in culture (like school activities on a "church" night), your family (like marriage or kids), and church (like an assembly schedule change) precipitate the need for further organization. No worries—you have the tools to reorganize.

"I am missing a receipt from your last trip. Do you know where it is?"

Even the most organized youth minister receives messages like this every once in a while. Still, this type of communication makes me nervous, perhaps because it draws out my insecurity of appearing unorganized. The difference today compared to the past "lost money bag caper" days? I know exactly where to look to find the receipt. I am much more organized.

CONCLUDING TRUTH: ORGANIZATION MATTERS.

OUTREACH
MATTERS

"Everything has changed. There is no ministry to the 'core group' anymore!"

The student who said this was one of our best and was going through a bit of a culture shock. The insider loop of relationship building in our youth ministry was being challenged, and a call was issued to look outside the usual loop. Students were asked to look beyond school, activity, and socioeconomic lines and create a "safe place" (that was our code term) in which everyone would feel comfortable and welcome to pursue a relationship with Jesus and his people.

"What's wrong with that?" you ask.

Well, when outreach works, the "others" begin to show up. "Others" are those who are not of the core group. They hover in the shadows during youth group, they sit by themselves in worship, they attend very few or no activities, and they, who can be churched or unchurched people, think of themselves as outsiders. But when outreach is taken seriously, when church becomes a safe place in which the usual rules of teenage demarcation[1] are willfully and strategically broken, magic happens! The others are brought into the core.

The student who said the opening quote in this chapter would be embarrassed at what came out of his mouth. It was a moment of frustration, and I understood. Actually, I took the comment as a wonderful indication that the insider loop was beginning to break. Oh, and the teenager who spoke those words? He is now working fulltime to bring others to the Lord.

TRUTH: OUTREACH MATTERS.

WHY?

Outreach matters because it matters to the Lord. In the armed forces, a commander's last order is the standing order of operation until that order is changed by the issuing commander or a higher-ranking commander changes the order. Jesus issued a standing order:

> Then Jesus came to them and said, "All authority in heaven and on earth has been given to me. Therefore go and make disciples of all nations, baptizing them in the name of the Father and of the Son and of the Holy Spirit, and teaching them to obey everything I have commanded you. And surely I am with you always, to the very end of the age" (Matt. 28:18–20).

> He said to them, "It is not for you to know the times or dates the Father has set by his own authority. But you will receive power when the Holy Spirit comes on you; and you will be my witnesses in Jerusalem, and in all Judea and Samaria, and to the ends of the earth" (Acts 1:7–8).

The order to do outreach has not been changed. Therefore, while we take care of, encourage, and strengthen those who are among us, we are to have our eyes on others as well.

Again, this was the witness and example of Christ.

> Jesus said to him, "Today salvation has come to this
> house, because this man, too, is a son of Abraham.
> For the Son of Man came to seek and to save the lost"
> (Luke 19:9–10).

Jesus spoke these words to Zacchaeus, an "other," and invited him into the core group by calling him a son of Abraham. Powerful words. They serve as an example of what youth ministers should be doing for the teenagers in their communities and youth ministries. Dangerous words. Jesus's behavior of taking others and making them core was one of the leading causes for his execution. These words are still dangerous; a youth minister can lose her job when the core does not want to make room for the others.

Think about the times when Jesus was angry. What made him angry? Jesus was angry when the practices of the core prevented the others from coming to him.

I believe that this still angers our Lord. Outreach matters to the Lord, and it should matter to his youth ministers.

HOW?

I believe most youth ministers have a heart for outreach—it is in our DNA. We have a reputation for going to extreme measures, from eating goldfish to shaving our heads, to draw a crowd in order to share the gospel.

However, outreach is more than a gimmick, and is difficult to sustain as a ministry focus. Even though used in some youth ministry circles, the following outreach activities are ineffective.

Bait and switch. This involves conducting an activity that draws a crowd and then delivering an unexpected gospel message. An example of this would be inviting students to watch a comedian (the bait) only to put the Jesus squeeze [2] on them at the end (the switch).

Outreach number nights comprise programming that encourages students to bring friends to reach a certain number, and then the youth minister will eat a goldfish, shave his head, or give everyone a trip to Disneyland.

"Ineffective? Are you kidding me?!"

"But we are drawing great crowds, and kids are coming to Jesus left and right."

But are the teenagers staying? Are the others integrating into the core? Teenagers seek authenticity, not gimmicks. Youth ministers will always look for and develop creative ways to do outreach. So if you invite students to watch a comedian, tell your guests beforehand that you are going to share the gospel. And if you want students to invite their friends, throw away the number goal and goldfish-eating gimmicks and fire up your students' passion to reach their friends.

We all have a heart for outreach. Consider the following when fulfilling Jesus's standing order in your youth ministry.

Outreach is a lifestyle, not a program. Jesus did not have a designated outreach program time in his ministry. Jesus was the program. So are his people. Read how the apostle Peter talked about this truth:

> But in your hearts revere Christ as Lord. Always be prepared to give an answer to everyone who asks you to give the reason for the hope that you have. But do this with gentleness and respect, keeping a clear conscience, so that those who speak maliciously against your good behavior in Christ may be ashamed of their slander (1 Pet. 3:15–16).

These words were written to Christians living in a world quite like ours today. In broader context, Peter was calling for Christ followers to live a holy life that draws attention, and then to use that attention to speak about the hope we have in Jesus. In youth ministry terms, when students and adults create a safe place for teenagers, it creates attention and attraction. No one wants to be a part of a youth ministry (or church, for that matter) when they feel that they are not seen or wanted. Step one: speak of, teach, and demonstrate outreach as a lifestyle.

Program for outreach. As Christians live an outreach lifestyle, it is strategic and helpful to provide programming assistance for believers to share their hope in Jesus. I have come to believe, especially in postmodernity, that inviting someone to church is a second move. In other words, once you have the attention of someone by the witness of your life and by developing a relationship with that person, then invite them to church.

Normal assemblies. Put yourself in the newcomers' shoes. Once invited to your youth ministry, do they know what to do when they arrive (check in, location, food service options, where to hang out before class, etc.)? Is there someone looking

out for them (visitor team, adult leaders, etc.)? Do they understand the language of church (salvation, sin, grace, morality,
etc.)? Where do they sit during assembly or small group time?
How do you obtain their information? How do you follow up
with them (text, email, card, etc.)? Are the students and adults
friendly and accepting of others?

We have all experienced this, but especially in the life
of a teenager, there is nothing worse than feeling alone in a
crowd. What can you change to improve your program to welcome others?

Special assemblies. Youth ministers are creative and can program some incredible outreach events. Go ahead and bring in
a magician, host a concert, create and eat the world's largest
sundae, host a battle of the bands, hold a basketball tournament,
create a special outreach night using *Halo* as a metaphor (that
one was fun, but we had to convince the adults we were not
playing on the "mature" rating). Just be authentic and up front
in declaring your intention to share the gospel! Also, don't get
so caught up in counting audience size that you forget that the
students in your ministry are your greatest outreach program.

Practice outreach. You have taught and inspired your students and adults that outreach is a lifestyle, and you have
programmed your normal and special assemblies with others
in mind. Now, as the youth minister, practice outreach in your
own life. Jesus said to those who followed him, "Come, follow
me . . . and I will send you out to fish for people" (Matt. 4:19).
The followers of Jesus were great at outreach because they did
what he did. If your students and adults do what you do, would
there be any outreach happening in your student ministry? Ask
yourself these difficult questions:

* In your assemblies, do you spend the majority of your time seeking out the "others" or seeking the core students and adults?
* Do you rationalize why you spend the majority of your time with a certain type (athletic, artistic, renegade, etc.) of student or adult in your ministry?
* Would people speak of your ministry like that of Jesus's? Were you available to the "least of these" (Matt. 25:40)?

To be clear, all types of students need your ministry. These questions are presented to help keep our focus on the Lord's standing order.

 ## NOW?

Outreach is important to the Lord and should be important to his people.

Evaluate. Take that walk through your student ministry and ask yourself those difficult questions. Get others involved with the evaluation and question-asking (youth team, trusted volunteer, or minister). Conclude with these questions:

* Is your youth ministry a safe place in which everyone feels comfortable and welcome to pursue a relationship with Jesus and his people? Why or why not?
* What do outside teenagers, churched and unchurched, think about your youth ministry?

Teach. Spend time teaching your students and adults about the reality of being lost (heaven and hell basics, social and emotional pain of teenagers) and the heart of God to find and restore the fallen. Inspire them to be the outreach plan of our Lord!

Raise the standard. Challenge and then expect your students to be rule breakers of teenage demarcation and to assist in creating a safe place for all teenagers. Challenge your adults to lead the way!

"They would miss me."

The teenager did not seem to fit in with this group of guys. The young man was a product of a rough background and had very little to offer in the way of teen "credentials." He was not an athlete, musician, or academician. He was not wealthy. He was, well, average. Still, every week, without fail, he sat between two members of teenage "royalty": athletes, attractive, class favorites.

I knew the answer but had to ask: "Johnny, why do you come to church every week?" Without hesitation, he said, "Because Tim and Sam would miss me." He was correct. They would have, and they kept on Johnny to attend every assembly and activity of our youth ministry.

What made the two young men royalty was not their impressive "credentials," but their impressive passion for outreach. That is why the young man's answer brought me to tears. These two core kids had made room for the other.

CONCLUDING TRUTH: OUTREACH MATTERS.

PHYSICAL HEALTH
MATTERS

"Beware of church potlucks!"

These words of advice were shared with me over a heavy, calorie-laden, fajita meal by an old preacher who took an active interest in my education toward becoming a full-time minister. It was the last in a series of lessons that involved gems of pastoral wisdom and the purchase of a dress shirt and two cool neckties. The ironic part of this last great lesson was that the man was overweight.

"Don't end up like me," he lamented. His disregard for health was cutting short his energy and effectiveness as a minister. He also felt that others judged him because of the extra weight he carried.

I showed empathy, but did not want to totally share in his lament. To be honest, what could I say? It was rather awkward. I thanked him for his advice and gifts throughout the day. I also told him that I would beware of church potlucks and assured him that I would pay attention to my health. It may not look like it at times (I love my red meat), but taking care of my physical health is something I have been attempting to stay on top of for close to thirty years now.

Disclaimer: I am not suggesting that youth ministers bow at the altar of powerlifting, cross-fit training, marathons, or the latest workout video craze. I am also not advocating a certain body type to qualify one for ministry to teenagers. However, I am highlighting the importance of striving to maintain a healthy lifestyle in one of the unhealthiest vocational ministry positions in the church.

TRUTH: PHYSICAL HEALTH MATTERS.

WHY?

Our physical health serves as a witness to a watching world. Any conversation on the physical health of Christians often leaves people feeling awkward, uncomfortable, and defensive. The conversation can derail quickly. For instance, the Bible condemns gluttony, and teachers automatically make the jump to overweight people (the two are not always related). Balance is a word we should remember when talking about a Christian's physical health. Context is also important to keep in mind.

> But the LORD said to Samuel, "Do not consider his
> appearance or his height, for I have rejected him.
> The LORD does not look at the things people look at.
> People look at the outward appearance, but the LORD
> looks at the heart."(1 Sam. 16:7).

> Do you not know that your bodies are temples of the
> Holy Spirit, who is in you, whom you have received
> from God? You are not your own; you were bought

at a price. Therefore honor God with your bodies
(1 Cor. 6:19–20).

For physical training is of some value, but godliness
has value for all things, holding promise for both the
present life and the life to come (1 Tim. 4:8).

Each of these verses has been used in the discussion on the physical health of Christians. Each provides a balanced insight and comes from a specific context.

In the context of selecting a king for Israel, the Lord reminded Samuel that physical health does not equate spiritual health.

In the context of avoiding sexual sin, Paul reminded his readers that a Christian's mortal body is a house for the divine.

In the context of teaching godly behavior to Christians, Paul reminded Timothy that spiritual training has superior value to that of physical training.

Nowhere do you read that unhealthy people are disqualified from ministry activity. You also do not read that it's permissible to embrace unhealthy choices. Perhaps there is a different angle we can take in the physical health conversation.

Live such good lives among the pagans that, though
they accuse you of doing wrong, they may see your
good deeds and glorify God on the day he visits us
(1 Pet. 2:12).

Yes, there is a context to address. Peter was calling Christians to live in such a way, among a judgmental world, that we authentically represent our Father.

Witness. Our lives are a witness to the transformative power of Christ at work in our lives. It stands to reason that our physical health is a part of our witness. Remember the word "balance."

More than likely, the majority of you reading this chapter struggle with some aspect of your physical health. You may struggle with overeating, over-caffeinating, overstressing, over-relaxing, and over _____ (fill in the blank). How you work on your physical health "overs" communicates a loud message concerning what you turn to and how you work on other struggles.

A more balanced approach is to view our physical health as part of our witness to the work of Christ in our lives. I believe that is what my old preacher friend was attempting to tell me all those years ago.

Extra truth. It takes a lot of energy to keep up with teenagers. You cannot be expected to keep your high school or college performance levels, but you can be expected to be an active participant in a round or two of Take a Hike or Bun Shuffle.

HOW?

Physical health is a matter of daily discipline. Again, there is a context to the following verses, but each one of them mentions the need for intentionality in maintaining a healthy lifestyle:

> "I have the right to do anything," you say—but not everything is beneficial. "I have the right to do anything"—but I will not be mastered by anything. You say, "Food for the stomach and the stomach for food, and God will destroy them both." The body,

however, is not meant for sexual immorality but for the Lord, and the Lord for the body (1 Cor. 6:12–13).

Therefore, since we have these promises, dear friends, let us purify ourselves from everything that contaminates body and spirit, perfecting holiness out of reverence for God (2 Cor. 7:1).

After all, no one ever hated their own body, but they feed and care for their body, just as Christ does the church (Eph. 5:29).

I will go ahead and say it, out loud: "It can be a real downer to live a healthy lifestyle!" Here's a little personal secret: I actually love me some McDonald's on youth trips (any trip, actually). I learned long ago that drivers eat for free when they bring a group of students into their restaurant. I feasted and capped off many a youth trip stop with a hot apple pie. As I get older and as the "responsible" calorie intake continues its journey downward so my waist will not expand outward, letting go of the hot apple pie is a bummer. Regardless of my feelings, if I want to remain physically healthy, I have to make disciplined and intentional choices in my eating and other areas of my life. I am not a health guru, nor do I want to present myself as someone who can provide medical advice, but I can share a few things that can help you maintain your physical health amid the pizza, Cokes, late nights, and long days of youth ministry.[1]

Get a yearly physical. It is important to know the health of your outside and insides. You may look great on the outside, but the standard blood work that comes with the yearly physical can let you know your real health score. Yep, that score was what ended my McDonald's visits.

Get moving. With all the activity of youth ministry, why do I need more movement? Because of cardio and flexibility. A youth minister can spend a great amount of time sitting and staring at a computer screen every day. As with all limited mobility jobs, it's important that you get moving.

Take the stairs.

Walk around your office or building when making calls.

Walk to nearby appointments.

Get up and do some intentional stretching (you may want to close the office door).[2]

Make good food choices. You do not need to eat the greasiest, cheesiest, bacon-filled red meat item on the menu (that sentence made me hungry). Most eating establishments provide healthier baked, white meat, turkey bacon options on their menu (I am no longer hungry). Youth ministry food is typically not healthy food. Be smart. Instead of eating six pieces of pizza, eat two pieces and a salad. Instead of drinking a six-pack of soda while driving, drink one soda and a few bottles of water. Balance is the key.

Get on a regular exercise plan. Before you buy that gym membership or purchase the latest exercise program or equipment on QVC, spend time thinking about what works for you. What type of plan will you enjoy enough to continue when the going gets tough? I train with a friend at a gym because I know that friend will encourage (or shame) me when I miss workouts. I need that competitive encouragement. I walk with my wife regularly because it is a constant source of cardio and opportunity for relationship building. By the way, we have a piece of workout equipment sitting in our bedroom that rarely gets used.

Get rest. Your body, mind, and spirit need to rest. Take a day off every week (it is called Sabbath, and it is in the Bible). Take your vacation (never leave vacation days on the table). Turn your phone off (it is a great interrupter of time and space). Sleep in when you need the rest. If you go and go and go because you feel the world will fall apart if you rest, you have other issues that need to be addressed. Rest!

 ## NOW?

Youth ministers are keenly aware that their students remain at the same age year after year while they continue to age and race toward oldsville. They understand that physical health matters if they want to remain in youth ministry for the long haul. Start making healthy decisions today.

Make the appointment. Schedule a yearly physical. Schedule a visit to a nearby gym. Schedule a time to visit with a friend who can keep you accountable to your physical health goals.

Start. As with any lifestyle change, starting can be the most difficult. Starting can be intimidating and the challenge can seem too impossible to conquer. Even so, make the decision to start your journey. Most of us know what we need to do to improve our physical health. Review the practical steps given above, gather advice from a trusted advisor, check out helpful websites, or follow the recommendations given from the appointments you made. Start!

Do not give up. There are many ups and downs, twists and turns, and victories and challenges on the road to physical health. Setbacks are expected. Don't give up.

"Mom, someone has been eating my chips!"

I could have remained silent and let my son take the fall, but I was the guilty party. I took the chips my daughter was planning on taking to school for her lunch. I literally took food from my own child. In my defense, they were barbecue-flavored and delicious!

I ate the chips because it was the end of a long day, I was tired, I was alone (everyone was asleep), and I felt like I deserved those chips. This is the greatest physical health challenge I consistently face. The long day, tired, alone, and "I deserve this" eating cycle loads the body with calories that aren't going anywhere fast. Oh, the high cholesterol loves those late-night eating cycles as well. Thus, I need to make a daily, intentional decision to limit my late-night calorie intake.

I do remain determined to improve and work on my health. I want to be healthy enough to continue the long haul of youth ministry. I also want to do my part in staying around for my wife and kids.

CONCLUDING TRUTH: PHYSICAL HEALTH MATTERS.

RELATIONSHIPS
MATTER

"God, I don't want to be alone anymore!"

These are the words written on a watercolor painting that hangs in my office.

The painting was given to me as a gift from a young lady who felt invisible in her school and family, and in the eyes of the watching and judging world. She was overweight. Silent. Uncomfortable. Outside. Sad. A cutter. Confident that God had forgotten about her.

Then she answered a friend's request to come to our youth ministry.

I wish I could tell you she had an amazing and miraculous night of response to the teaching. Or that she was suddenly grabbed by the amazing decor, worship, and light show on stage. On the contrary, while she did appreciate the youth ministry event, it was the way she was welcomed by students that began and accelerated her journey out of solitary confinement. That acceptance opened her heart to the worship and teaching, and subsequently led her to write these words on the back of that same sad and desperate watercolor painting:

Dear Dave,

This painting may not seem like a lot, but it means a lot. I never really believed in God until a few weeks ago. It confused me; it scared me, the idea of him. I didn't think that I was worthy of something or someone who would love me no matter what. Who would accept me for who I was. Besides that, I had gone through things that just totally made me think there was no way that he was real. Still, I prayed one single prayer every night hoping that someone was listening. That prayer was, "God, I don't want to be alone anymore." I prayed that single prayer for as long as I could remember, and finally, a few weeks ago, I found that I wasn't alone. I was introduced to a home. A place where I was accepted for me, where I was loved.

The note was signed and dated, with this added:

"P.S. Today marks my one month since I last hurt myself. I'm hoping next month is my second."

TRUTH: RELATIONSHIPS MATTER.

WHY?

God created us in and for relationship with him and each other.

From the creation narrative to the Revelation of John, this truth is seen throughout Scripture:

The LORD God said, "It is not good for the man to be alone. I will make a helper suitable for him" (Gen. 2:18).

I will take you as my own people, and I will be your
God (Exod. 6:7a).

Now this is eternal life: that they know you, the only
true God, and Jesus Christ, whom you have sent
(John 17:3).

If one part suffers, every part suffers with it; if one
part is honored, every part rejoices with it. Now you
are the body of Christ, and each one of you is a part
of it (1 Cor. 12:26–27).

And I heard a loud voice from the throne saying,
"Look! God's dwelling place is now among the people,
and he will dwell with them. They will be his people,
and God himself will be with them and be their God"
(Rev. 21:3).

We were not created to live life alone. God placed in each of his
creation a desire to be fully known and fully accepted. Then
why are relationships so difficult? The Fall.

Adam and Eve were convinced by Satan that the path to
being fully known and fully accepted was to become their own
boss. Well, how did that work out for them?

They no longer wanted to be fully known—they covered
their nakedness. They no longer found full acceptance—they
were banished from God's paradise. Yes, through Christ, God
covers our nakedness and restores our presence in paradise.
Even so, a defeated and evil Satan continues to offer humankind
the same path and promise. And how is that working out for us?

We cover our nakedness with attitude, activity, and accomplishments—multiple masks hide a fully known identity. We search for paradise in possessions, passions, and people, with full acceptance always beyond reach.

Instead of delivering paradise, like the young lady I shared about, many find themselves on the edge of chaos and collapse as they are unable to constantly deliver the needed "products" to gain relational acceptance. There is another way!

HOW?

God fully knows and accepts us, and does so through the fully known and fully accepted sacrifice of Jesus. We know of and experience the reality of this truth by the testimony of the Holy Spirit and in relationship with God's people.

> Because you are his sons, God sent the Spirit of his Son into our hearts, the Spirit who calls out, "*Abba,* Father." So you are no longer a slave, but God's child; and since you are his child, God has made you also an heir (Gal. 4:6–7).

> Dear friends, since God so loved us, we also ought to love one another. No one has ever seen God; but if we love one another, God lives in us and his love is made complete in us (1 John 4:11–12).

The Spirit does its part in acknowledging and helping us embrace the reality that we who were once unacceptable slaves to sin are now acceptable sons and daughters of God. John reminds us that the experiential reality of that truth is found in the way God's people relate with one another. In other words, the way we practically love and live in community with each other is intended to reflect and draw others into love and community with God.

While important, the events of youth ministry in and of themselves do not possess the life-changing power often bestowed on them by youth ministers. The events possess life-changing power to develop and support relationships with God's people. The relationships are what matter.

The Fuller Youth Institute found that students who have meaningful relationships with parents and youth ministers (professional and volunteer) and are welcomed into relationship by their church community possess a higher probability of "sticky faith" (a faith that is external in action, internal in devotion and motivation, personal, communal, mature, and maturing).[1] In other words, students who feel they are fully known and fully accepted by these significant adult players receive and keep the faith better than students who feel they have to hide their "nakedness" from adults and/or perform well enough to be welcomed into adult "paradise."

All youth ministry programming, from worship to water balloons, should keep in mind that relationships matter. Parents, youth ministers, and every member in the church community have a responsibility in relationship development.

Parents are to be viewed as partners, not problems. Parents, positively or negatively, are primary, not secondary, spiritual influences in a kid's life. Parents are to be encouraged and treated as primary players.

Youth ministers are to view themselves as cultural missionaries who assist students in being fully known and fully accepted by the church. Youth ministers are to view and speak of volunteers as coworkers, not sponsors. (Not all students will connect with you, the "professional"—get over it.) Youth ministers are to view each program as an opportunity to connect students in meaningful relationships with God, adults, and other students.

Church communities are crucial players in a student's spiritual formation. Church community programming, directly or indirectly, is youth ministry programming. Church communities are to be encouraged and trained to be student ministry partners. From learning and pronouncing a kid's name properly to inviting students into an adults-only church activity are practical steps that come from first understanding and then embracing the significant role adults play in a kid's spiritual formation.

It is not a suggestion. It is a command. "Impress them on your children" (Deut. 6:7a). It's not just a command for youth ministers. It's a directive given to all of God's people.

 ## NOW?

By trade, youth ministers are typically great relationship brokers. You understand that relationships matter. Broaden your message and influence.

Start the conversation. You may want to share this chapter as a starting point with your senior pastor, church staff, ministry team, parent committee, or class. Talk about the significance of relationships in your training sessions, teaching, preaching, and those casual coffee conversations. These conversations lead to the buy-in that programming change can and should occur to strengthen relationship development and growth.

Change something. It does not need to be big, but it does need to be significant. In other words, don't go into the senior pastor's office and demand that students lead the Sunday morning worship team. Instead, ask a few senior adults to join you for class and give their testimony. Or change your vocabulary from "sponsor" to "coworker" on your volunteer applications and explain the change at your next training session.

Share the story. Big or small, a change produces a story. Brace yourself—it could be a not-so-friendly story. Regardless, a story emerges, the sharing of which will serve as a motivation for more change or as a reset button to try another programming move. Whatever the media—spoken, written, video, or audio— share stories. They are the fuel of motivation and an avenue of accountability for church leaders.

Repeat. Keep going. Remember, "change is a small rudder on a big ship and takes time."[2]

I recently received a text from a local care provider who specializes in working with high-school-age students. The text was urgent (names have been changed):

> "I have Drew in my office. Is there a time you and
> your friend can come and talk to him? He's acting
> pretty desperate."

I know the student's story. He is afraid of being fully known and does not feel fully accepted by the significant adults in his life. It is a dark, sad, and all-too-familiar tale shared by many teenagers.

Why text me?

I have a friend who shares the same dark, sad, and familiar narrative, but arrived, many years ago, on the other side of the challenge. My friend's story will help this young man imagine and begin writing a different story for his own life. We are providing an opportunity for a fully known and fully accepted relationship to develop.

The program being suggested by the care provider is clear, and the student will have to accept the invitation. The program is a person.

CONCLUDING TRUTH: RELATIONSHIPS MATTER.

RETREATS AND CAMPS
MATTER

"I will remember that event for the rest of my life!" were the words spoken by several of my high school youth group kids and adult volunteers.

Every lesson, activity, and free-time moment was designed to lead up to this one capstone learning activity. The event was rather simple and involved blindfolds, loud and conflicting messages being given by adults, and plenty of time.

Youth ministry magic. It worked!

The processing that followed the activity lasted more than an hour. The statements given by both student and adult participants solidified the feeling that the capstone event was a success:

"This was so real-life for me."

"I never realized how difficult making the right decision can be."

"The person I trusted lied to me."

"I will make better decisions with my life from here on out."

"I am in a bad place and need prayer."

"My influence has much more impact than I had thought."

"Following Christ is extremely difficult."

"My life is going to be much different when I return home."

To this day, if you were to assemble the students and adults that attended that weekend retreat, I am certain they would say, "I will remember that event for the rest of my life!"

Youth ministry magic, indeed.

In my opinion, in all youth ministry programing, the weekend retreat and camp programs are among the most impactful.

TRUTH: RETREATS AND CAMPS MATTER.

 WHY?

There are moments in which the routine of spiritual activity, going to church, is in need of fresh insight and a renewal of purpose. When the mundane has captured the miraculous and the depressed lays siege to the dynamic, a retreat (weekend retreat or weeklong camp) is in order. Retreats provide a time of strategic rest and refitting so that lives can be resumed with renewed strength and determination. Many Bible characters took times of retreat after an upsetting challenge or failure.

> When Pharaoh heard of this [Moses killing the Egyptian], he tried to kill Moses, but Moses fled from Pharaoh and went to live in Midian, where he sat down by a well (Exod. 2:15).

> Elijah was afraid and ran for his life [Jezebel wanted to kill him because her prophets were dead]. When he came to Beersheba in Judah, he left his servant there, while he himself went a day's journey into the wilderness (1 Kings 19:3–4a).

When they had finished eating, Jesus said to Simon
Peter [after his denial and moment with the resurrected
Jesus], "Simon son of John, do you love me more than
these?" (John 21:15a).

Other people from the Bible experienced retreat moments in
order to gain fresh insight or a renewed purpose.

Now when Joshua was near Jericho, he looked up
and saw a man standing in front of him with a drawn
sword in his hand. Joshua went up to him and asked,
"Are you for us or for our enemies?" "Neither," he
replied, "but as commander of the army of the LORD
I have now come." Then Joshua fell facedown to the
ground in reverence, and asked him, "What message
does my Lord have for his servant?" The commander
of the LORD's army replied, "Take off your sandals,
for the place where you are standing is holy." And
Joshua did so (Josh. 5:13–15).

But when God, who set me apart from my mother's
womb and called me by his grace, was pleased
to reveal his Son in me so that I might preach
him among the Gentiles [Paul's conversion from
persecutor to persecuted], my immediate response
was not to consult any human being. I did not go
up to Jerusalem to see those who were apostles
before I was, but I went into Arabia. Later I returned
to Damascus. Then after three years, I went up to
Jerusalem to get acquainted with Cephas and stayed
with him fifteen days (Gal. 1:15–18).

> Then Jesus [after his baptism by John] was led by the
> Spirit into the wilderness to be tempted by the devil
> (Matt. 4:1).

> From that time on Jesus began to preach, "Repent, for
> the kingdom of heaven has come near" (Matt. 4:17).

The retreat activities of some of these greats lasted for years, and for others, days. Regardless of the time span, they made an intentional break in their routines so that a spark of renewal could ignite into a strategic refit for battle.

A battle looms on the horizon. But for this day, rest.

HOW?

Like the greats above, retreats can be assigned or placed upon an individual. In today's youth ministry world, retreats and camps are strategic go-to activities. Here are a few things to keep in mind when planning a weekend retreat or weeklong camp session.

Work the "Four S" approach for planning. Here's an approach that can help you plan retreats quickly and effectively. It is also easy to remember, which is a definite plus.

Strategy. What do you want your students to leave with? Purpose. How will they get it? Planning. Great retreats and camps do not just happen—they are planned. You have to spend time strategizing what your students need and how you plan to get them what they need. A whiteboard and sharp group of adult youthworkers who have listened to the needs of your students and actual teenagers can help with this process.

Schedule. More than likely, unless you are camping or staying at a private property, there will be set times for meals and major activities (rope courses, pool, etc.) at your location. Operating within this framework, schedule your programming so that the purpose of your event can be fulfilled. A good rule of thumb is to be sure you end your retreat with tangible, practical, and easy-to-take-home action items. In other words, don't end with an emotional high that is impossible for them to maintain when they get home. Bring your students down off the mountaintop and into the valley of reality. Also, be creative with your teaching time. Don't be afraid to go big with an active learning experience.[1]

Staffing. Bring plenty of adult youthworkers on the retreat or camp. As long as they have a job and are productive (I realize that can be subjective), the more the merrier.[2] Also, be sure to ask your event venue what their student-to-adult ratio is for overnight lodging.

Safety. Liability and medical release forms, nurse/first-aid care and a medication delivery system, conflict/crisis management, disciplinary procedures, travel arrangements, and code of conduct and rules while at camp are all examples of safety concerns that must be addressed well before the event arrives. If you are unclear of your church's safety procedures, ask. If you don't know what is appropriate for medical care, ask. If you are unclear of your transportation safety protocol, ask. The reasonable assurance of safety allows both parents or guardians and students to relax and get the most out of the retreat experience. If a student does not feel safe, whether physically or emotionally, it is almost impossible for them to grow spiritually. You may want to underline or highlight that last sentence (be sure to read the Safety Matters chapter for more quick-start suggestions).

Plan the right amount of free time. Free time is important to build community in your ministry, but too much of a good thing can turn bad quickly. Too little free time and students get restless. Too much free time and students may miss the intended spiritual direction of the retreat. Again, strategy and schedule are in relationship with each other. Though often at an additional cost, your venue may provide some extra activities (paintball, canoeing, archery, etc.).

Be careful with competitive games. Our teenagers live in a world of competition. This may seem like an overstatement to adults, but just ask a teenager. Almost everything they do is analyzed and presented for judgment. They need a break. So instead of making every free-time activity a team competition, play games that place all students on an equal footing and that strengthen group cohesion. If you are so competitive you can't think of any such games, check out *Best-Ever Games* and *Awaken Your Creativity* by Les Christie. He is the game guru in youth ministry.

Rest. This may make the youth minister unpopular, but do not stay up too late or wake up too early during retreat weekends and weeklong camp sessions. It is better to return your students (and adults) rested for their upcoming week. Also, be responsible with a student's emotional state when talking about deep, eternal, and life-altering topics. In other words, if feasible, have a conversation that has the potential of an emotional charge during the day hours.

Don't be a "schedule jerk." You made the schedule and can change the schedule. If students are processing an activity and going deep into the purpose of your event and the next scheduled activity is free time, change the schedule. Don't rush so fast into the next activity that you jerk the students' emotional chains.

Be responsible with emotions. It can be easy to manipulate a student's emotional state. Be responsible. Be careful. A student's tears do not necessarily indicate that you are fulfilling your retreat's purpose. "I cry, therefore I am saved," is not an accurate measure of student growth.

Building relationships and memories is key. Your students will not be able to recall all that was taught at your retreat or camp, but they will remember key moments. Those moments will revolve around key experiences that impact them deeply. Experiences will be different for every participant, so don't shortchange any phase of your schedule planning.

A well-planned strategic retreat or camp is a sharp tool in a youth minister's programming toolbox. Retreats and camps can:

* Launch a new ministry focus.
* Renew a student's understanding of the gospel.
* Expand a student's understanding of key theological concepts (Sabbath, grace, service).
* Encourage students to impact the world around them.

Retreats and camps can serve as moments of spontaneous transformation in which a student's spiritual life is forever changed by a single, powerful moment.

NOW?

Most of you reading this have a retreat weekend or weeklong camp looming on your program horizon.

Work the "Four S" approach. Create some space in your schedule to work through the process. Better yet, invite key leaders to join in the discussion.

Release your creativity. Once you have your purpose, get lost in the plan. Go to that place where no idea is a bad idea, and create! An incredible and original teaching idea may surface. Or, explore, refine, and contextualize how others have addressed your retreat or camp purpose.

"Hey, we are not supposed to be on our computers!"

As I write this chapter, I am getting heckled by students and adult youthworkers because I am on an actual youth retreat and the topic is Sabbath rest. As I write, I am witnessing rest, relationship and memory making, carefully scheduled free time (which we are currently enjoying), and lives being impacted for eternity.

Students will return from this retreat ready to advance with fresh insight and renewed purpose. Youth ministry magic. It worked.

CONCLUDING TRUTH: RETREATS AND CAMPS MATTER.

SAFETY MATTERS

"Hey, get off the top of that car!"

After a Tuesday night Bible study during my first year of youth ministry, these words flew out of my mouth as I stepped outside my house and saw a kid standing (surfing, actually) on top of a moving car.

Two thoughts immediately went through my head as I shouted these words. One, the "surfing kid" is reckless and that driver is extremely irresponsible. Two, I am now a grown-up, and I may or may not have participated in such activities during my teenage years.

Okay, there was also a third thought: I am so getting fired if that kid gets hurt at my house.

I am certain the pressure and concern for students' safety weighs heavily on the hearts of all youth ministers. In many ways, youth ministry has an inherent risk involved with each activity: travel, backpacking, work projects, lake activities, ocean activities, ski trips, athletic activities, slip and slides, water balloon fights, retreats, camps, mission trips, lock-ins.

Risk is part of any youth ministry. The above is just a small list of activities from my thirty years of student ministry in which risk became a reality and safety measures were brought into action.

From students on cars to students in the hospital, you will experience it all. Be prepared.

TRUTH: SAFETY MATTERS.

WHY?

Unless you are a reckless youth minister, there is little need to answer this question.

Youth ministers should feel the heaviness of their responsibility. To be clear, I am not suggesting you become paralyzed by fear and wrap your students in bubble wrap. Such activity damages students (a topic for another day). I am suggesting you take steps to minimize risk and have a plan to respond when a crisis does occur because safety matters. Consider the following.

You are given the responsibility to care for a parent's son or daughter. I have always understood this reality but did not fully feel that responsibility until I had children of my own. It is a big deal for parents to feel safe, comfortable, and confident when allowing their children to participate in youth programming.

You will be looked to for leadership when a safety crisis occurs. You will experience a safety crisis moment. It is unavoidable. Be prepared.

You will be held responsible. As a leader, whether it is your direct fault or not, you will own what happens in your youth ministry. It is imperative that you do your job of minimizing risk and that you have a plan in place to respond when a crisis occurs.

These realities are enough to sober up the most reckless of youth ministers. While we work toward minimizing risk, it is unrealistic to think that safety can be guaranteed. Adults cannot make such promises. Our world is filled with trouble.

> The LORD is a refuge for the oppressed, a stronghold in times of trouble (Ps. 9:9).

> If you falter in a time of trouble, how small is your strength! (Prov. 24:10)

> Remember your Creator in the days of your youth, before the days of trouble come (Eccles. 12:1a).

> I have told you these things, so that in me you may have peace. In this world you will have trouble (John 16:33a).

Even though I have worked hard to minimize risk in my student ministry, I have had to respond to trouble. Broken bones, bloody noses, sexual misconduct, drug use, psychological breakdowns, heatstroke, physical threats, and death (suicide, accidental, and natural) have all been troubles that I have had to respond to in my youth ministry. Youth ministers must be prepared to respond when safety has been stripped away.

HOW?

It is possible to minimize risk and prepare for crisis in youth ministry. Disclaimer: The following is not an exhaustive list of all that can be done to minimize risk and prepare for crisis. However, it will get you heading in the right direction and provide helpful, quick-start reminders.

Standing policies and procedures. Depending on your ministry context, most churches have policies and procedures in place to minimize risk and respond during a crisis. If you have not done so already, ask for those. Familiarize yourself with and implement those policies and procedures.

Starting from scratch. If you do not have safety policies and procedures in place, get them in place quickly. Start with your church's insurance company. It would also be helpful to enlist the assistance of volunteers who work in education, law (both judicial and enforcement), and medical fields.

Color inside the lines. Guidelines and instructions are given for almost any activity you and your students will be involved in. Driving, camping, team-building courses, adventure rides, water activities, etc., are all examples of activities that have posted guidelines and instructions. Listen to and follow that information.

Background checks. These are not optional for anyone working in your youth ministry. Do not compromise on this step.

Be the adult. Like the story at the beginning of this chapter, you are responsible for making sure that students (and adults) color inside the lines. That means you will need to discipline people and hold them accountable for unsafe behavior. It's better to be safe than cool.

Be prepared. Do you have all you need to safely conduct the program? Food, safe vehicles, medical and other types of release forms, water, beds, medical supplies, life jackets, harnesses, helmets, etc., are examples of needs that will be taken into account when planning an activity.

Trust your gut. If you have a feeling that something is unsafe, follow your gut. That instinct, which could quite possibly be a prompting from the Holy Spirit, is most often correct.

My mind is flooded with memories in which each of these risk-minimizing suggestions came in handy and saved a troubled situation from going over the edge into crisis.

Prepare for Crisis.

Forms. It is important that you have both a liability form and medical release form on file for each participant. Check with your church's leadership about requiring a separate release form for each overnight or high-risk (e.g., ropes course, high-impact athletic, day hike) activity.

Currency. Depending on the crisis, be sure you have access to enough currency (cash, check, credit, or check card) to get the situation under control.

Medical supplies. Be sure you have a stocked and updated medical kit with you at all times. It is a great idea to get a medical professional to take responsibility for preparing and maintaining this resource. They can help you plan for all contingencies (preparation for a zombie apocalypse does not count). And be sure you have duct tape on hand.

Mechanical supplies. If you have your own vehicles, what happens if you break down? Have a flat? Have a wreck? Be sure you have a decent tool kit with you. Also, I learned this from a near fatal failure, be sure the tire jack that came with your vehicle actually provides safe usage.

First-aid training. Get trained on the basic elements of first aid. If you can obtain advanced training, get that as well. You will use such training more than you can imagine.

Adult volunteers. Be sure you have enough volunteers who understand that they too have a responsibility to keep students (and adults) coloring inside the lines. It is a special bonus, and is required by some camp and retreat centers, to have a registered medical professional as part of your volunteer adult staff.

Plan ahead. Spend time thinking through every possible scenario of risk for each youth ministry activity. Remember that not all safety risks come from the outside. Mental and emotional safety are items you need to plan for as well. I am not asking you to be paranoid, but I am asking you to be prepared.

Remain calm. Even in the most chaotic of crises, remain calm. Remember, whether you wanted it or not, the adults and students are looking to you for direction and support. Slow down your processing and give clear, decisive instructions.

Youth ministry programming safety will remain a constant and ongoing concern of parents, church leaders, and participants.

You will have anxious, unrealistic parents. Be patient.

You will have noncompliant, risk-taking volunteers. Be firm.

You will have unexpected trouble come your way. Be prepared.

 ## NOW?

Trouble will find its way into your youth ministry. What do you need to do now to minimize and prepare for the risk?

Commit to safety. Youthworkers pray that students will open up and be transparent about their need for Christ, godly relationships, and instruction. If a student feels unsafe (emotionally, physically, or spiritually), they will not risk such vulnerability. A commitment to safety helps parents, volunteers, and students commit themselves wholeheartedly into ministry programming. Once the feeling of safety is lost, it is difficult to bring back. Commit to minimizing risk and preparing for crisis.

Systems check. How safe is your youth ministry? Using the above suggestions, ask yourself these questions:

* Do I have and use liability, medical, and event release forms?
* Do I typically have liability, medical, and event release forms for each of my program participants?
* Do I have any adult volunteers that are not background-checked?
* Do I have a stocked and current medical kit?
* Are my church vehicles safe to drive?
* If a crisis hit my youth ministry (death, accident, injury), am I (and my team) confident or prepared to meet that challenge? Why or why not?
* Do I color inside the lines? Do my adult volunteers?

If your dashboard trouble light lit up on any of these questions, it's time to get to work.

"I will remember this day for the rest of my life!"

On May 2, 1999, I was driving a bus of teenagers returning from a weekend retreat when the nightmare of every youth minister became a reality. On a mountain road, a truck pulling a fifth-wheel trailer came across the center line and cut its way through the left side of my bus. Seven precious lives ended on that day (six from our church and one from a following vehicle), and several were seriously injured. Everyone involved in that tragic day carries scars.

Even when risk is minimized, tragedy may strike. Be prepared.

CONCLUDING TRUTH: SAFETY MATTERS.

SELF-CARE MATTERS

"David, I want to thank you for the example and mentor you are to me."

This compliment was interrupted by my flood of awkward, snot-producing, exhausted tears. I had been in full-time ministry for six years, and I was moving fast, too fast! No exaggeration, I was:

Leading a youth ministry (with all that this involves);

Preaching every other week (my church was without a preacher);

Coaching football at a local high school;

Teaching adjunct college courses;

Playing on at least two intramural teams at the university;

Playing on a youth group indoor soccer team (shout-out to the Slugs!);

Accepting the occasional speaking gig;

Oh, and being a husband to Lisa.

I was standing in the lobby during the National Conference on Youth Ministries (NCYM) when the compliment was given. I had left the meeting room because the message had rocked my world and convicted me of my lack of self-care, and I felt exposed. That particular NCYM was the first youth ministry conference I had ever attended. It is not that I had a problem with the conference—I simply did not see the need for taking a break and failed to recognize that my pace of ministry was unhealthy and needed an overhaul.

That is why the compliment led into an awkward, snot-producing, exhausted tears moment. That moment, resulting conversations, and practical corrections started a career-saving shift in the way I practiced youth ministry.

TRUTH: SELF-CARE MATTERS.

WHY?

Youth ministers need to take care of themselves before they can adequately take care of others. Every time we get on a plane, we are told to place the oxygen mask on our own faces before assisting those around us. Jesus, the one we follow and attempt to imitate, put the self-care oxygen mask on first.

> When Jesus heard that John had been put in prison, he withdrew to Galilee (Matt. 4:12).

> When Jesus heard what had happened, he withdrew by boat privately to a solitary place (Matt. 14:13a).

> Yet the news about him spread all the more, so that crowds of people came to hear him and to be healed of their sicknesses. But Jesus often withdrew to lonely places and prayed (Luke 5:15–16).

When the apostles returned, they reported to Jesus what they had done. Then he took them with him and they withdrew by themselves to a town called Bethsaida (Luke 9:10).

Jesus, knowing that they intended to come and make him king by force, withdrew again to a mountain by himself (John 6:15).

Jesus withdrew, a lot. Youth ministers know this truth. This is what we teach our students, right?

We tell students:

* If they want to hear from God, turn off the noise of the world.
* Solitude and rest are spiritual disciplines needed in their busy schedules.
* God created the Sabbath for a reason, and that reason is their well-being.

I did not practice great self-care in the first years of my student ministry. It almost destroyed my desire to be in youth ministry (my marriage was also beginning to suffer). I had a problem—I had a messiah complex. You can find various definitions for this, including in psychological journals, but in youth ministry terms, I felt indispensable to all that was going on in "my" youth ministry. They needed me and I needed them (and the affirmation they gave me). I had to fix all their problems. I had to comfort their pain. I had to teach all their classes. I had to answer all their cries for help. I had to be their "messiah."

My youth minister tried to tell me I was not the messiah. But I continued on with my "messianic" pace of life until that moment at NCYM and my realization of the actual pace of life of the actual Messiah. Jesus withdrew. He rested. He took in the oxygen of his Father before assisting those around him who were suffocating in need of life-giving oxygen.

HOW?

If you do not plan for and make self-care a priority, it will not happen. You may experience periodic lows in activity, but most teenagers and families (and youth ministers) are one step away from a crisis. There will never be a perfect time to withdraw from people and practice self-care, but withdraw you must or you will not last long in youth ministry. Because they are different, I will break this section into daily, weekly, and yearly categories.

Daily. Every day of the week can have a different rhythm for a youth minister. Some days are filled with activity prep, others with lesson prep, and others with pastoral visits. Some days you finish knowing that you did something but can't really remember what happened. Youth ministers inherently love the unique challenge each day brings. Self-care, as we see in the life of Christ, demonstrates a daily calm amidst the chaos. Even if only for a moment, make it a priority to:

Pray. Talk to the Father. Also, learn how to sit in silence and listen to him.

Read. Read the Bible and some other book that fosters spiritual growth (this does not entail reading for lesson prep!).[1]

Work. At times, a youth minister's lack of self-care is a direct result of his lack of work ethic while in the office. Plan and execute your tasks with excellence. Procrastination creates undue stress on you, your family, and your church.

Rest. Get your work done and go home. Go to bed at a decent hour so you can wake up at a decent hour.

Turn off. Get away from your phone and computer. If you do not, self-care is impossible in today's social media environment. If there is an emergency, it will find you.

Weekly. The weekly category has always been my biggest challenge in self-care. Take your day off! Do you remember all those Sabbath day verses in the Bible? You could be killed for breaking the Sabbath (there is a pretty good chance that many reading this book would be dead by now if that law was being enforced today). We live in a culture (and church culture) that applauds runaway activity and looks down on those who take a weekly break. In youth ministry, you will often be asked to watch a game, eat lunch, or grab a coffee. It becomes easy to fill your day off with just one game, lunch, or coffee. Protect the day! Here are some helpful tips for having a great day off:

* Turn off your phone.
* Do not check or update social media.
* Sleep late if you can, or nap during the day if you can't.
* Go out to eat (if you have a spouse, take your spouse out to eat).
* Do something you enjoy (a hobby, a movie, a book, a visit with a friend, etc.).
* Stay away from the church building and from those you minister to regularly.

Yearly. There are a few things you need to be sure to do every year.

Take your vacation. I have been guilty of not using all my vacation time. That is an awful thing to do to yourself and your family. If you can't afford to go anywhere, then plan a staycation.

Practice all the day-off tips during these extended periods of rest.

Attend conferences. More than likely, you will be given time and resources to attend at least one conference a year (if not, your leadership needs some education in minister care). After the emotional moment described at the beginning of this chapter, I have not missed an opportunity to attend a professional youth ministry conference.

Take some time. Most youth ministers possess a great deal of flexibility in their schedule. Take a day or two to get away and reflect on your own spiritual life, ministry, and strategic direction. This type of activity can be strengthened by a visit with a trusted mentor or friend.

Ministry is fluid, and a crisis does not wait to be invited into anyone's schedule. The best of self-care plans will shift, just as they did for Jesus. Don't worry—just get back on track as soon as possible. Remember, place the oxygen mask on your own face first.

 NOW?

Self-care begins with a choice. It really is that simple (I did not say easy). You have to make the choice to take care of you. If you don't, youth ministry will make the choice for you, and you will be on the fast track toward burnout.

Evaluate. How is your level of self-care? Open your calendars (youth, personal, family) and ask yourself these searching questions:

* Are you taking your day off? The entire day off?
* How is your prayer life?

* Are you doing any personal reading?
* What are your peers telling you about your ministry pace?
* What are your spouse and family saying about your ministry pace?
* Are you in control of your social media involvement? Can you turn off your phone?
* When was the last time you took a vacation?
* When was the last time you went to a class without teaching?
* Do you feel that your schedule is out of control? Is this because your work ethic needs work? Or have you developed a messiah complex?

Don't despair—all youth ministers will find an area or two needing improvement they when evaluate their level of self-care.

Practice. Make the choices to strengthen your daily, weekly, and yearly self-care. To ensure your practice matches your desire, accountability is key. Ask and then allow your spouse and peers to hold you accountable to a balanced ministry lifestyle.

Seek professional guidance. There may be a moment or two when you sense the need to visit with a counseling professional. Drop the pride and make the appointment! Youth ministers refer students and adults to counselors all the time. Sometimes we need to refer ourselves.

The NCYM message that rocked me and pushed me outside the meeting area was actually the concluding illustration used by the speaker. The speaker talked about his love for hot tubs and about a moment at a hotel in which he had to choose whether or not he would sit in a dirty, leaf-filled, unclean hot tub. After a long day on the road, he really wanted to enjoy that tub. So he ignored the dirty condition by pushing the whirlpool action button. The bubbles created from the disturbed water concealed the gross condition of the tub. The speaker then made the powerful connection that many of us were ignoring the dirt and exhaustion in our own spiritual lives because we keep pushing the button of youth ministry activity.

I wanted to push the button, so that's why I left the room. But instead of reaching for the whirlpool action button, God sent a friend with a compliment. I was convicted and broken.

Now, I have learned to periodically stop and clean my ministry with self-care. Now, when the whirlpool of ministry action button is pushed, the water is fresh, clean, and enjoyable.

CONCLUDING TRUTH: SELF-CARE MATTERS.

SEXUAL PURITY
MATTERS

"The greatest number of pornographic movies are rented during youth ministry conferences."

This statement was made at the National Conference on Youth Ministries (I recall a similar statement being made at the National Youth Workers Convention as well). The discovery did not come through a systematic research process. The truth came from the hotel staff itself! They found it curious that out of all the conferences they had hosted, youth ministers bought the most porn. Wow!

What followed was an open and honest dialogue about the struggle for maintaining sexual purity in the life of a youth minister.

"David, can I talk to you?" a youth minister said with a shaking voice.

"Sure, what's up?" I responded.

The youth minister broke down into tears and said, "I am struggling with porn."[1]

This type of conversation has been repeated over and over again in my ministry. Even though difficult, I love these moments because they indicate the person is ready to take sexual purity seriously. It is a holy moment in which a sacred trust occurs because access is being granted into the darkness residing inside the heart. It is also a moment of honor as the light of grace and spiritual direction is poured into the brokenness.

Let's set the table a little more for this chapter. They may be out there, but I do not know the name of a youth minister (any minister for that matter), male or female, including myself, who has not struggled against, struggled with, or continues to struggle with sexual purity at some level. Satan is crafty. In my experience, those who accept, prepare for, and bring their struggle into the light of accountability are much more successful in their commitment to sexual purity. However, those who minimize the challenge and fail to prepare often find themselves in situations they never could have imagined.

I am not writing this chapter to frighten church leaders into keeping their youth ministers away from conferences. I'm writing this because youth ministers, male and female, must take sexual purity seriously.

TRUTH: SEXUAL PURITY MATTERS.

 WHY?

Human sexuality is a powerful and wonderful gift from God, a gift that should be enjoyed and protected. Scripture is clear about keeping sexuality pure.

> Drink water from your own cistern, running
> water from your own well. Should your springs
> overflow in the streets, your streams of water in the
> public squares?

Let them be yours alone, never to be shared with
strangers. May your fountain be blessed, and may
you rejoice in the wife of your youth. A loving doe,
a graceful deer—may her breasts satisfy you always,
may you ever be intoxicated with her love. Why,
my son, be intoxicated with another man's wife?
Why embrace the bosom of a wayward woman?
(Prov. 5:15–20)

You have heard that it was said, "You shall not commit
adultery." But I tell you that anyone who looks at
a woman lustfully has already committed adultery
with her in his heart. If your right eye causes you to
stumble, gouge it out and throw it away. It is better for
you to lose one part of your body than for your whole
body to be thrown into hell. And if your right hand
causes you to stumble, cut it off and throw it away. It
is better for you to lose one part of your body than for
your whole body to go into hell (Matt. 5:27–30).

Marriage should be honored by all, and the marriage
bed kept pure, for God will judge the adulterer and
all the sexually immoral (Heb. 13:4).

I often ask students to respond to a series of uncomfortable questions.

"Who made sex?" I ask.

"God," they respond.

"Who wants you to have the best sex life?" I ask.

"God," they respond.

This is how I typically start my "sex talks" with student
groups. It is a much more positive approach than what I heard
growing up from youth leaders. The "sex talks" I received were

awkward and were delivered with a more threatening and fear-filled tone.

"If you have sex before you are married, you will get pregnant, get a disease, or die and go to hell!" or something like that.

"If you think about sex or about seeing a member of the opposite sex naked, you may die and go to hell!" or something like that.

"If you ask any questions about human sexuality, we will think you are a pervert or sexually active!" or something like that.

Yes, I exaggerated a little bit. The point is that we must start with the positive. Scripture is filled with words that honor human sexuality and speak of it as a powerful and wonderful gift from God to be enjoyed and protected.

HOW?

Because of its complexity and intensely personal nature, the topic of sexual purity can wander in a number of different directions. My purpose here is to present the most foundational and effective methods I have found to assist youth ministers in maintaining their sexual purity.

Choice. As a youth minister, whether you are single or married, woman or man, young or old, full time, part time, or volunteer, you must first make the choice to keep and maintain sexual purity. Give God, not contemporary culture, the authority to dictate how you will honor and manage your sexual desires.

Accountability. We were not made to journey through life or youth ministry alone. Certainly, husbands and wives have a covenant accountability to sexual purity. Still, especially when pornography is involved, spouses can quickly drift into isolation and dark shame. It is wise for youth ministers to have someone outside their marriage and of the same gender (that should be a no-brainer) who will hold them accountable to sexual purity. This person should be given the authority to ask difficult questions, possess the ability to be blunt and rebuke when needed, and give helpful direction. In other words, they need to love you enough to tell you what you need to know, not what you want to hear. Also, they can tell on you and get you busted if necessary. That's accountability. Who is that person of accountability in your life?

Consumption. What you listen to, watch, and read impacts your ability to maintain sexual purity. To the single, if you choose to one day be married, a lack of sexual purity in your media consumption will affect your future marriage intimacy. To the married, just because you have a sex life doesn't mean you no longer have to safeguard your media consumption. The media that married couples consume, together or privately, also affects their sexual intimacy and expectations.

* Do you pay attention to media ratings for television, movies, and video games?
* Do you set parental codes on your televisions so that you cannot channel surf onto an inappropriate channel?
* Do you inform your accountability partner when you are on a trip that involves a hotel stay so he or she can hold you accountable as to what you watch in the privacy of your room?
* Do you have a magazine subscription that needs to be discontinued?
* Do you have accountability software on your various media devices?[2]

Have you ever wondered why the magazines and books are organized the way they are in airports, convenience stores, and bookstores? It is so the eye will be attracted and the purchase, or at least the browse, is made. Be careful of your consumption.

If you are a breathing human being, you are attracted to beautiful and desirable things. This is especially true of our sexuality. We must watch the object of our attention. Advertisers use sexual tension to get our attention. That is why they use all those supermodels (men and women) to pitch the sale of cars, coffee pots, toothpaste, toenail polish, and more—it works!

> Above all else, guard your heart, for everything you
> do flows from it. Keep your mouth free of perversity;
> keep corrupt talk far from your lips. Let your eyes
> look straight ahead; fix your gaze directly before you.
> Give careful thought to the paths for your feet and be
> steadfast in all your ways. Do not turn to the right or
> the left; keep your foot from evil (Prov. 4:23–27).

To the men. Kenny Luck of Every Man Ministries came up with the attention strategy of "bounce and bless." The strategy, designed specifically with men in mind, acknowledges a man's God-given desires while also holding that gift accountable. Bounce the eyes (attention) and bless (pray for) that which drew your attention (this may be obvious, but it's typically not a head-bowed, out-loud prayer type of thing).

Let's try out the strategy: When walking through a public place, do your eyes get drawn to a certain part of a woman's body? Bounce the eyes away from that body part and ask the Lord to bless that woman's day.

Get it? It's rather simple, and it works. Bounce and bless.

To the women. Ladies, your attention must be brought into accountability as well. The bounce and bless method may work for your visual attention temptations; however, as my wife has pointed out to me, this attention challenge is often more personal for women. A woman's desire to receive someone's special affection is God-given. In addition, that desire for affection can draw a woman's heart and corresponding actions in a direction she never felt possible. Often, the story of sexual purity failure in youth ministry is told from the male perspective. Yet there are plenty of stories of brokenness that are told from the female perspective. Women must also guard the focus of their attention.

To the married. One more word on "attention" for married youth ministry couples: if there is anyone or anything drawing your attention away from your spouse, get away from it! I cannot emphasize this enough.

Knowledge. Remember, Satan is crafty. He knows exactly when a sexual purity temptation will be most appealing to you. He knows when you are tired, feel unappreciated, and feel like you deserve a little thrill. He knows when you are feeling unattractive, unnoticed, and in need of a little attention. He knows when you are stressed and need a little distraction from the realities of life. Like Eve's conversation with the serpent, he knows you, youth minister. Be prepared. Knowing when you are most vulnerable is a valuable key to maintaining sexual purity.

Scripture gives us excellent advice on how to deal with Satan and his temptations: "Submit yourselves, then, to God. Resist the devil, and he will flee from you" (James 4:7).

NOW?

The youth minister's fight to maintain sexual purity never ends. It is a noble and good fight that will strengthen your own sexual relationship and add great credibility to your ministry. It's important that we are a little unnerved by this so we will be prepared. A compromised sexuality leads to broken marriages and damaged credibility. Keep fighting.

Forgive yourself. If your sexual purity is in shambles, start with forgiveness. The Lord forgives and restores people—that is what you teach. Believe and accept his love. Often the greatest challenge in restoring sexual purity is the shame that accompanies such failure. The process of forgiveness is done in community and involves confession. The depth and breadth of community confession can be a delicate matter for a youth minister, who is often a public figure. The questions of "Who should know my struggle?" and "How much should I tell them?" are best answered with a trusted and wise church leader and/or accountability partner. Whether privately or publicly and regardless of the lack of comfort and pain, sexual sin needs to be confessed and forgiven.

Get to work. Do the things that help you maintain your sexual purity, today! Start practicing the how's, or find other how's that will assist you in your fight for purity. One of the best places to start is by finding or talking with your accountability partner. Go ahead, make that call or send that text. Arrange a meeting in which you let that person into the darkness or potential darkness of your heart. Give them permission to journey with you as you practice the discipline of sexual purity.

Get help. Talking about sexual purity can be a Pandora's box. If you find yourself in need of professional help, I beg you to get the help you need. If you don't know where to start, call someone you trust to point you in a helpful direction (perhaps your accountability partner can assist you).

"I need you to put parental codes on the TV!"

I was a little nervous when I made this request to my wife. Even though a little scary, she was glad that I did, and affirmed my decision to be as safe as possible with my channel surfing. That small decision has helped my sexual purity a great deal throughout the years. I love historical war documentaries and movies. Often these are R rated for their graphic content. Even though I have to call my wife to unlock such channels, it is worth it. The conversation I have with her on why I want a certain channel unlocked keeps me out of trouble.

CONCLUDING TRUTH: SEXUAL PURITY MATTERS.

TEACHING MATTERS

"God comes first, run away, surround yourself with good people, remember your commitments, and I'm a winner!"

Now a college student, the young lady ran up to me on a university campus and excitedly recalled all five points of a lesson I had given years earlier. As a teacher, this was an incredible moment of affirmation! A student not only remembered a lesson, but recalled all the points. Wow! The responsibility of teaching is a joy.

"David, you need to check your facts before talking about youth culture."

This young man was angry that I had negatively talked about his favorite band and got all the facts wrong. He was right. I did not do my homework, and I really blew the illustration and corresponding point. As a teacher, this was an incredibly humbling and embarrassing moment. It was also an awakening. Students were actually listening to my teaching. I had to be sure what I was saying was biblically and culturally accurate. Wow! The responsibility of teaching is a heavy burden.

If you have done any amount of teaching with teenagers, I am certain you can relate to both of these stories. One moment, you are on top of the world, and the next, your heart is in the pit of darkness and doubt.

You can count on one thing when teaching teenagers—they will let you know how they feel.

TRUTH: TEACHING MATTERS.

WHY?

Youth ministers know that teaching matters. That is why most search out the best curriculum, listen to other speakers, and make a habit of constantly writing down all types of potential illustration ideas on napkins, note cards, and smartphones. It's not just the delivery youth ministers care about, it's the weight of responsibility.

> If anyone causes one of these little ones—those who believe in me—to stumble, it would be better for them to have a large millstone hung around their neck and to be drowned in the depths of the sea (Matt. 18:6).

> In the presence of God and of Christ Jesus, who will judge the living and the dead, and in view of his appearing and his kingdom, I give you this charge: Preach the word; be prepared in season and out of season; correct, rebuke and encourage—with great patience and careful instruction. For the time will come when people will not put up with sound doctrine. Instead, to suit their own desires, they will gather around them a great number of teachers to say

what their itching ears want to hear. They will turn their ears away from the truth and turn aside to myths. But you, keep your head in all situations, endure hardship, do the work of an evangelist, discharge all the duties of your ministry (2 Tim. 4:1–5).

Teaching is a heavy responsibility.

I believe that youth ministers are some of the most creative teachers in the church. However, it is important that they stay grounded on this truth. It is the message, not the method, that changes lives.

> When I came to you, I did not come with eloquence or human wisdom as I proclaimed to you the testimony about God. For I resolved to know nothing while I was with you except Jesus Christ and him crucified. I came to you in weakness with great fear and trembling. My message and my preaching were not with wise and persuasive words, but with a demonstration of the Spirit's power, so that your faith might not rest on human wisdom, but on God's power (1 Cor. 2:1b–5).

Why do we teach? To make Christ and his kingdom agenda known. That is why youth ministers work on and care so much about how those teachings are delivered.

HOW?

It is very tempting for a youth minister to put the "how" before the "why" of teaching. We see something creative (video, activity, story, song, etc.) and want to fit it into a teaching that does not fit the context of Scripture. Be careful—here is why I start this section with this truth.I was a sophomore in college and taking my first homiletics class, and I really thought I was nailing the semester. I had prepared and delivered great lessons, or so I thought. Then, one day after class, my professor, Charles Stephenson, caught me and said these words that I have kept close for thirty years: "David, you have the gift of gab. Be sure you study!"

I do not think I'm alone in this admonition. Many youth ministers are naturally gifted with the "gift of gab," so we have to work to keep the "why" before the "how."

My purpose in this chapter is not to talk about youth ministry curriculum options, as there are a number of great products available. My concern is that you have the ability to deliver lessons that you have developed from your own study with your ministry context in mind. If you can do that, then you can use and adjust any curriculum to fit your youth ministry.

Here are a few quick-start suggestions.

Know the purpose of your teaching. Are you preparing a sermon, class, seminar session, or devotional message? The process of preparation can be similar, but each has its own uniqueness to consider. In other words, a sermon typically lasts twenty to thirty minutes, a class lasts forty-five minutes to an hour, a seminar is a series of thirty-minute to ninety-minute classes, and a devotional message lasts for ten to fifteen minutes. Here are some other purpose questions to consider:

* Is this a prophetic teaching (calling people to action or a course correction) or pastoral teaching (comforting, encouraging, or instructing people)?
* Is this a one-time teaching or a teaching in a series?
* Is this teaching reactive (in response to an event), or proactive (in preparation for an event)?

❊ Is this an exegetical (centered around one particular section of the biblical text) or topical (making use of various biblical texts but centered on addressing a particular topic) teaching?

Know the content. Again, drawing from the words of my mentor: know the material! Put in the work to ensure you are using the biblical text correctly. Put in the work to check and recheck your sources. No, you cannot be an expert in everything, but you can be as prepared as possible when delivering a message to those who will take your words (and tweet them) as truth.

Focus the message. This is the hardest part of teaching for me. After studying, I typically have a lot of content to pare down into edible chunks. There have been times when a great teaching has become just a fair to good teaching because of too much content. I have a mentor who reminds me of this truth by saying, "David, great teaching, but you took them through the cafeteria line too many times."[1] Focusing the message is particularly difficult when preparing a one-time message. Regardless of the tedious and difficult process, refine your content into easy-to-present and memorable morsels of truth.

Add creativity to the message. This is the part of teaching in which you pull out the video, activity, story, or song you have been saving on that napkin. A good rule of thumb is to use one creative element to illustrate each point of your message. However, you are the one creating the content, so use what you feel best supports the truth you are wanting to bring to your audience's attention. The purpose, content, and focused message should inform what type of creativity you will utilize. The demographics of your audience should also inform the creative elements of your message.

Decide how you will launch and land the message. Once the content of your teaching is complete, go back and develop your introduction (launch) and conclusion (landing) elements. I would love to say that the launch and landing always come after the content is complete, but in reality, how you decide to begin and end your message may become clear as you go through the above process. Because of its importance, let's look at the launch and landing separately.

Launch. Get the attention of the audience with your opening comments—this is the "hook" of your teaching. Audiences quickly decide if they want to tune in or tune out within the first few moments of a presentation. Therefore, nervous chatter, taking too long with thank-you comments, and other forms of pre-message talking can tune out an audience. My advice, unless absolutely unavoidable, is to get into your teaching quickly. Starting with a story that draws the audience into your message or drawing them in with a question are great ways to launch. If in doubt, simply read the key biblical text on which you will focus your message. The point is get the audience on board and to launch your teaching quickly.

Land. You have shared the content. Now, land the plane. What do you want your audience to do with the message? What is the biblical text calling your audience to do with the message? The type of action you call for depends on the purpose of your teaching. Once an action is chosen, the smooth landing needs to bring your audience to the ground with a clear understanding of what they should do with what they just heard.

Develop your delivery. You will develop, if you have not already, a "notes" or "no notes" style of teaching. You will also develop a "walker" or a "one-place stander" style of presentation. In your delivery, I recommend that you focus on clarity of speech, passion for your content, authenticity in your concern that the audience receives the message, and confidence demonstrated in your body language. If you really want to advance your delivery, listen and/or watch one of your lessons (I find this rather painful, but productive), or ask an accomplished teacher to critique your message and delivery (don't be defensive). All of us have had that favorite teacher we would attempt to imitate in our delivery, but my hope is that you will work on finding your own unique delivery style. That is the one God gave you—use it.

It has always been helpful for me to go back and look at the various teachings of Jesus and the apostles. You will see most, if not all, of the above principles at work in these instances.

 NOW?

Youth ministers reading this chapter may have an upcoming class or seminar to prepare. Many will know exactly what they will be teaching—that makes the development and delivery of the message more manageable. However, there are others who have no idea what they will be teaching. This leads to a frantic search to find something (story, video, song, etc.) that can be used to form a message. If you find yourself in the second category, the following quick-start tips are for you. Note: Students typically know when you are just throwing things together.

Find out what your students need to receive from your teaching. After the frantic search for "something" is over, take some time by yourself, with a team of youth ministers, or with your volunteers, and ask, explore, and discuss the answers to these strategic questions:

* What are the demographics of your youth ministry (family stability, private or public school, high- or low-income, athletic or artistic, biblically literate or illiterate, etc.)?
* What are some of the major challenges facing the young people who live in your community, go to local schools, and attend your church? (If you don't know, ask them.)
* What are some of the concerns you have when thinking about your students and families?
* Does your youth ministry have an atmosphere in which students can doubt and ask and explore difficult questions? Why or why not?
* What do you want your students to know before graduating from your youth ministry?

You can and should add questions that you feel are more contextually relevant. The challenge is to develop a teaching plan that is strategically beneficial to your students. This process ensures that your lessons have a trajectory and purpose.

Practice before you preach. Before your next lesson, try out the process and see if it helps you develop and deliver a higher-quality message.

"This is the Bible I carried in high school."

I am a sentimental guy and have kept items, many of which now reside in my attic, from all my years of participating in and leading youth ministries. Two of the items I keep on my bookshelf are the Bibles I used in high school. I periodically pull them off the shelf and show them to students. What I see in the text and margins are markings and comments from lessons now long past that remind me once again how much teaching matters.

CONCLUDING TRUTH: TEACHING MATTERS.

VOLUNTEERS MATTER

"We need to find three more adult volunteers or we cannot stay overnight at the retreat site."

I heard this from my admin on the Monday before the Friday the retreat was scheduled to start (this is also the day that I discovered the "overnight rule" of students-to-adults ratio in the state of Texas, 1:10). I was in a bind.

Up to this moment, my wife and I, with the occasional interested adult, would load up our handful of students and travel all over "doing" youth ministry. That seemed to work well when our ministry was small, but our group was growing. That is a great thing, right? Not if you are a superhero youth minister.[1] To be clear, I have always respected and made use of adults in my youth ministry, but I haven't always used them very well in my youth ministry (e.g., retreats and summer camps).

I had to find three adults quickly or the retreat was off. So I put the superhero persona away and changed the way I thought about and conducted a retreat.

Guess what? What I found was amazing! The execution, depth, long-term impact, and fun was increased tremendously by involving more adults in my youth ministry.

TRUTH: VOLUNTEERS MATTER.

 WHY?

Youth ministers need to invite adult volunteers into meaningful and impactful ministry. If you think of adult volunteers as support staff for your ministry, it is time to rethink your role as a youth minister—you're not as important as you think you are (ouch!). Christian Smith and Melinda Lundquist Denton discovered that the top and close second influencers of a student's spiritual formation are parents and the surrounding adult community. Youth ministers and youth ministry programming are important, but are a distant third in significance.[2] This truth is found within the framework of Scripture.

> Hear, O Israel: The LORD our God, the LORD is one. Love the LORD your God with all your heart and with all your soul and with all your strength. These commandments that I give you today are to be on your hearts. Impress them on your children. Talk about them when you sit at home and when you walk along the road, when you lie down and when you get up. Tie them as symbols on your hands and bind them on your foreheads. Write them on the doorframes of your houses and on your gates (Deut. 6:4–9).
>
> Teach the older men to be temperate, worthy of respect, self-controlled, and sound in faith, in

love and in endurance. Likewise, teach the older women to be reverent in the way they live, not to be slanderers or addicted to much wine, but to teach what is good. Then they can urge the younger women to love their husbands and children, to be self-controlled and pure, to be busy at home, to be kind, and to be subject to their husbands, so that no one will malign the word of God. Similarly, encourage the young men to be self-controlled. In everything set them an example by doing what is good. In your teaching show integrity, seriousness and soundness of speech that cannot be condemned, so that those who oppose you may be ashamed because they have nothing bad to say about us (Titus 2:2–8).

Do you see it? These two scriptures have been used throughout this book to support and demonstrate why the use of adult volunteers is crucial to your youth ministry success. Parents and the surrounding adult community are expected to model what a follower of God looks like. This happens through formal, informal, by-word, and by-action teaching opportunities.

A superhero youth minister may bring in the occasional sidekick but is not utilizing the power of spiritual formation that can come from a fully employed adult volunteer.

Why do youthworkers continue to wear the superhero mask? Here are a few answers to that question:

Perception. Youth ministers may perceive the adults in the church as being uninterested in volunteering for the youth ministry. Or, adults in the church may have a perception that their youth ministers do not need or want them volunteering in youth ministry.

Time. It's easier to get things done yourself. That is, until your group starts growing and the needs increase. Time is needed to get adult volunteers equipped and ready to serve.

Arrogance. Youth ministers typically do a better job teaching and leading youth ministry activities. If not checked, ability leads to a "the students need me" arrogant mentality.

Whatever the reason, youth ministers must fight the urge to wear the mask and instead do the hard work of recruiting, training, and empowering adult volunteers.

HOW?

Recruiting, training, and empowering adult volunteers requires hard work, but the impact of a committed adult volunteer is vital to the success of a youth ministry.

Recruiting. I do not know of a church in which the perception that youth ministry adult volunteers aren't wanted is truly a reality. Often, the lack of adult volunteers is directly related to the youth minister's inability to recruit volunteers. Here is a list of tried-and-true volunteer recruiting suggestions:

Change your language. Speak of mission instead of task. A request to fulfill tasks (we need someone to drive the van, host the devotional, cook the food, chaperone the students, etc.) does not have the same weight as a request to join the mission (we need adults who want to impact the lives of the next generation). Speak of youth ministry volunteers instead of sponsors. A call for more youth ministry volunteers to join the team is much more appealing than asking for more sponsors (that sounds like a school-sponsored trip request). Speak of volunteers instead of chaperones. A volunteer chooses to serve within a group; whereas, the word "chaperone" indicates the need for someone to oversee rather than be an active participant. "Chaperone" also carries the idea that you are at an event to police teenagers' behavior. Students do not need another principal. They need a friend and mentor who has volunteered to be with them. Change your language.

Expand the pool. The first place many youth ministers go looking for volunteers is within their friend group. While this is a natural place to start, this pool of volunteers is limited and can lead to an insider club mentality that excludes would-be volunteers. It can also foster a narrow-sighted leadership vision in which no one is willing to offer "outside the box" opinions for fear of seeming disloyal to the leader. You can avoid these difficulties by looking for volunteers from other groups of people in your church. Cast a wide net when looking for volunteers.

Have a clear process and purpose. You have someone interested in serving in your youth ministry, so what's next? Have a clear process for processing and assigning volunteer positions. Is there a card, form, or web page to fill out? Is there a list of volunteer opportunities with job descriptions? When will they be contacted? When will they be trained? Put yourself in a volunteer's shoes, and prepare clear and purposeful documents that answer all their questions and launch them into service successfully.

Be honest. Just because they checked the "I want to teach" box does not mean they are gifted in that area of service. Be honest with your volunteers as they inquire about volunteering and explore their interests in the ministry. Work with them, but let them know you will discern where their talents fit best and can have the greatest impact. Be honest with yourself as well.

Often, volunteers may have a better up-front presence than you do. Yes, you are the leader, but be humble enough to share the stage with talented volunteers.

Training. Youth ministry volunteers are among the most valuable assets in a youth minister's toolbox. Tools need to be maintained and sharpened to remain useful for service, and they also need to be used according to their designed purpose. In a crunch, many of us have used the back of a wrench as a hammer, but valuable volunteers deserve quality training so that each volunteer uses his or her best gifts. Some training will be done one-on-one or in small groups. Several training sessions will be specific to a class or event preparation. The training suggestions below, while applicable to smaller event-based training, are given to provide direction for larger, all-in volunteer training events.

Set the expectation. Youth ministry volunteers are busy. If you want a good turnout, the date, time, length, and purpose of the volunteer training event should be set and communicated months ahead of the actual event (six months ahead is a good rule of thumb). Provide a snack or meal for your volunteers. Provide babysitting for those who need that service. These small steps communicate a high level of expectation for your volunteer team and gives them confidence that their time and participation is important and valued. Finally, and I cannot stress this strongly enough, never apologize for the time you are taking to train your volunteers. It devalues the training.

Give them something. Perhaps it is a special one-of-a-kind volunteer shirt, book, bag, or mug. These types of gifts build team morale.[3]

Communicate your vision and mission. Every gathering should include a reminder of the reasons behind what you're doing for teenagers in your youth ministry. Do not assume that people know the overall vision and mission of the ministry. Remind them, and let them know that they are key members of the vision and mission.

Give them a nugget from teen culture. Share an insight that helps your volunteers better understand the students they are serving. This could be a teaching from you, a video from an expert, or insights from a chapter or article.

Give a ten-thousand-foot view of the youth ministry. Like the president's State of the Union address, give your team an overview of the current state of the youth ministry. Numbers will be involved, but be sure to tell stories of impact. A great activity to follow your comments is to ask your volunteers to share stories from their experiences.

Give a five-thousand-foot view of the youth ministry. This is where you unfold the upcoming events in which your volunteer team will be involved in executing. Teaching series, special events, new programming, small groups, retreats, mission trips, and camps are all examples. There's no need to delve into deep detail.

Give a street-level view of student ministry. Not all five-thousand-foot items need to be given a street-level view. For instance, if a retreat is four months away, there is probably not a need to give a detailed view of that event at volunteer training. You decide what needs to be viewed from the "street." Depending on the size of your volunteer team, this step is best done in similar volunteer groupings (e.g., volunteers helping with teaching meet to discuss teaching, volunteers helping with small groups meet to discuss small groups, etc.). Each breakout should have specific action items and clearly defined next steps to accomplish.

Leave with a purpose. End the meeting with creativity and purpose. This can entail a time of focused prayer, a word of encouragement from a student, joining together in worship, or having your senior minister encourage and praise your volunteers. Be intentional. Leave your volunteers feeling refreshed, appreciated, and inspired.

Empowering. Once your volunteers are given a task and trained for it, empower them to do their job! That said, be careful not to fix every problem and/or take over when things are difficult. You may be equipped to handle the difficulty better, but if you do, you may pull the chair out from under them or make them dependent on your hand-holding. So, allow them to fail if necessary. Again, empower your volunteers to lead.

> So Christ himself gave the apostles, the prophets, the evangelists, the pastors and teachers, to equip his people for works of service, so that the body of Christ may be built up until we all reach unity in the faith and in the knowledge of the Son of God and become mature, attaining to the whole measure of the fullness of Christ (Eph. 4:11–13).

 NOW?

The need for recruiting, training, and empowering youth ministry volunteers never ends. Even if your numbers stay level, the need to find and replace volunteers will never go away.

Evaluate and correct. Evaluate your volunteer recruiting, training, and empowering processes. Ask these questions:

- Is the process for becoming a volunteer in your youth ministry clearly stated and understandable? If no, why not?
- Do you have volunteers without a job to do? If yes, why?
- Is it hard to recruit volunteers? If yes, why?
- Do your volunteers know the vision and mission of the youth ministry? If no, why not?
- Do you have volunteers that give off a "we don't need anyone else" vibe and keep others from serving in the youth ministry? If yes, why?
- Do you struggle with volunteer retention because you fail to empower? If yes, why?
- Do you struggle with volunteer recruitment because you are a superhero youth minister? If yes, why?

Now, start taking steps to correct any deficiencies.

Set the expectation. Plan your next volunteer training, and make it excellent!

"These are my kids!"

It took me a while to realize the hard fact that I would not be the most important adult youthworker in every student's life in my youth ministry. To be honest, it used to hurt my feelings when students would talk about other adult youthworkers on Senior Sunday and never mention my name. Now, I love it! I consider the fact that they are saying the names of other adult youthworkers a great success! That is why I love to hear my youthworkers say, "These are my kids!" Because they are.

CONCLUDING TRUTH: VOLUNTEERS MATTER.

WORSHIP MATTERS

"When peace, like a river, attendeth my way, when sorrows like sea billows roll . . ."

I mentioned earlier the event of May 2, 1999. I was driving back from a fabulous retreat weekend, and the bus I was driving was struck by a fifth-wheel trailer. The collision resulted in the heartbreaking loss of six wonderful young ladies and an older gentleman traveling behind our bus.

After the ambulance rides and emergency room visits, the surviving students who had been released from the hospital and adult volunteers gathered alone in a small youth room provided by a wonderful church in Alamogordo, New Mexico. The state police had just given me the final list of names of those we had lost and the plan to get my students back home to Lubbock. I carry the memory of their shocked and fear-filled faces with me this day.

I gathered myself, spoke the names clearly, and calmly explained that we would be boarding two buses to Artesia to meet the rest of our group and head home.

A tearful response came: "We are getting on a bus?!"

My wife, other adults, and I gathered around them and assured them we would be with them and that getting on a bus was the plan. It took a while, but we got on the bus.

I was the last to board. Assuring the kids and looking into their eyes as I passed, I finally made my way to the back seat and collapsed into my wife's lap.

With the exception of the sniffles and quiet tears, all was eerily quiet, until Justyn began to sing, "When peace like a river . . ."

Soon, those who had just experienced an unbelievable horror, leaving them speechless in their pain, worshiped. In fact, they worshiped and wept all the way to Artesia.

Worship invaded our pain, and we could breathe again.

TRUTH: WORSHIP MATTERS.

WHY?

Worship is a part of every youth ministry programming. Like teaching and preaching, it is one of the standard programming activities. Yes, worship is expected of the believer, but not as a work.[1] Worship, corporate and private, is a blessing that brings comfort, marks an event, provides focus, acknowledges pain, and unleashes power.

> Then David [after his son died] got up from the ground. After he had washed, put on lotions and changed his clothes, he went into the house of the LORD and worshiped. Then he went to his own house, and at his request they served him food, and he ate (2 Sam. 12:20).

After this, the Moabites and Ammonites with some of the Meunites came to wage war against Jehoshaphat. . . . Alarmed, Jehoshaphat resolved to inquire of the LORD, and he proclaimed a fast for all Judah. The people of Judah came together to seek help from the LORD; indeed, they came from every town in Judah to seek him. . . . As they began to sing and praise, the LORD set ambushes against the men of Ammon and Moab and Mount Seir who were invading Judah, and they were defeated (2 Chron. 20:1, 3–4, 22).

At this, Job got up and tore his robe and shaved his head. Then he fell to the ground in worship (Job 1:20).

About midnight Paul and Silas were praying and singing hymns to God, and the other prisoners were listening to them (Acts 16:25).

Therefore, since we are receiving a kingdom that cannot be shaken, let us be thankful, and so worship God acceptably with reverence and awe, for our "God is a consuming fire" (Heb. 12:28–29).[2]

Worship is not something you check off your list of things to do. There is power when we worship God—in pain, in crisis, in celebration, in fear, in praise, in doubt, in trouble, in comfort, in the assembly, in the car, in a room, in a jail, in a hospital.

Worship causes things to happen. Go back and read that verse about Jehoshaphat again. Worship is not only a defensive comfort—it is an offensive reality.

The purpose of this chapter is not to comprehensively address any worship war that may be present in your ministry context. The focus is on showing that worship matters in your youth ministry. Even so, I would like to give you three things to think about when addressing worship mode and style.

Context. Leviticus 10 (Nadab and Abihu), 1 Corinthians 14:40 (fitting and orderly), and similar worship verses have been taken out of context and used as ammunition to fire up opinions concerning mode and style. The richness of these verses has been lost by terrible exegesis. Beware of the context of the verses you use when talking about worship mode and style.

Love. Be careful not to judge another believer's motive or declare him or her "disfellowshipped"[3] because he or she practices a different mode and style of worship. In short, if you are quick to cut people off and declare them lost, keep this verse in mind:"We love because he first loved us. Whoever claims to love God yet hates a brother or sister is a liar. For whoever does not love their brother and sister, whom they have seen, cannot love God, whom they have not seen. And he has given us this command: Anyone who loves God must also love their brother and sister" (1 John 4:19–21). Love those who do not share your opinions on worship mode and style.

Understand. Raising hands and dancing around is not an indication of a true worshipper. Sitting on hands and steady feet is not an indication either. Clapping hands or not clapping hands. Shouting or whispering. Hymns or harmonies. Standing or sitting. Organs or keyboards. One worship song may move you to tears and do nothing for the person standing next to you. That is a normal and beautiful thing about the body of Christ. Seek to understand and honor your brothers and sisters in Christ. Be slow to judge.

Yes, there is much more that can be said to help navigate offensive worship discussions, but I want to end this short discussion with one statement: We will be held to account if we spend more time talking about worship than talking to the lost about Jesus.

Focus on the simple truths that worship does something and that our students need to be worshipping.

HOW?

It is an unfair assumption and expectation that all youth ministers know how to lead worship. Whether it is leading singing (a cappella) or leading a band (instrumental), this is an unfair quality many churches look for when hiring a youth minister. Some churches believe they are getting two for one in a hire when the youth minister can lead singing or a band.

So for some youth ministers, incorporating worship into youth ministry programming is in their wheelhouse. And for others? Well, they feel like they have been run over by a train when placed in a worship-leading situation. Here are a few quick-start suggestions for both groups of youth ministers:

Get help. Whether you know what you are doing or not, get help. Find those volunteers gifted in worship leading, share your vision of the importance of worship with them, and release them for ministry.

Get your students involved. Your students have talent—use them! Teenagers bring a refreshing level of passion to the stage when leading, passion at a level many may not consider "right worship." You know your church culture, so prepare them. I am also not suggesting that you use your students to push a worship mode or style agenda. If necessary, educate your students on the need to consider others before they lead.

Strive toward excellence. This should be obvious but needs to be stated. No one likes bad worship leading, which can be distracting. "Bad" is not necessarily tied to horrible vocals and playing—it can also be tied to presentation style. I do not want to be a reductionist, but you will know when excellence is present. In my opinion, if you run across a leader who thinks striving for excellence in worship is surrendering to consumerism, be patient. They may have a legitimate theological concern they need to work through with you. Or, they may be operating out of fear and anxiety. Either way, you will not know unless you seek to understand.

Remember the place and power of worship. Whether comfortable or not, get your students worshiping! Again, worship is not something to check off our programming list. Worship is essential.

Monitor emotions. Do not be afraid of emotion, but do not make it the marker of a successful worship event. Do not be afraid to use the emotion of a story or song to move the audience toward the understanding of truth. However, do not let the use of emotion outweigh the significance of the truth you are wanting to communicate.

Watch your words. Be mindful, theologically mindful, of what you say when leading your students (or church) in worship. Here are a few statements I hear often in worship gatherings:

> "Jesus, we welcome you into this place."
> "Jesus, come into this place."
> "Jesus, you are welcome in this place."

It sounds good, but is simply not accurate. Did Jesus leave? Unless unpacked, these statements sound more like incantations than a call to worship. Do not echo the words of the latest worship leader. Be careful with your words—your students are listening.

Add depth and breadth to your worship. Activities such as singing and speaking are often the focus of worship, which is so much more. Worship can happen in silence, in a reading, or in an observation of nature. Worship is also connected to lifestyle. Paul prompts, "Therefore, I urge you, brothers and sisters, in view of God's mercy, to offer your bodies as a living sacrifice, holy and pleasing to God—this is your true and proper worship" (Rom. 12:1). The point is to not relegate worship to a corporate activity on a stage—it's so much more.

 NOW?

Even though the depth and breadth of worship covers your daily life, more than likely you have a "stage" worship moment or activity planned for this week.

Prepare. God deserves our best. Have a plan and prepare to execute that plan. Has the worship leader prepared his team? Are the presentation slides prepared? Is the atmosphere of the room prepared (lights, stage, seating, etc.)? Do your volunteers know their roles? Do they know how to speak into a microphone? Are your worship leaders spiritually ready and able to give?

Pray. Pray for every element of your assembly (technology to music to venue). Pray for your leaders. Pray in the name and authority of Jesus Christ. Remember that powerful things happen when we worship.

Process. I got this suggestion from a group of great worship leaders: After the event, process with your team about successes and areas that need improvement. This is crucial for effective worship programming.

"When they had sung a hymn, they went out to the Mount of Olives" (Matt. 26:30).

Yes, the hymn closed the Passover meal, but we know what was coming for Jesus in that garden.

Did Jesus gain strength to make the journey to Golgotha from the hymn?

Did Jesus recall the words of this last song while he suffered?

Did the apostles recall the events of those dark days the next time they heard that hymn sung? I know that every time I hear the words "when peace like a river," I remember.

CONCLUDING TRUTH: WORSHIP MATTERS.

YOUTH MINISTRY MATTERS

"What is your defense for youth ministry in the local church?"

This question welcomes my students into the Introduction to Youth Ministry class that I teach. For some, what follows is a lesson in frustration.

Student: "The Bible says that no one should look down upon you because you are young."

Me: "Are you sure? Timothy was probably thirty or so years old!"

Student: "Jesus said, 'Let the children come to me.'"

Me: "Okay. What does that have to do with youth ministry?"

Student: "Teenagers don't want to hang with adults. They need someone closer to their age to lead them to Christ."

Me: "So, I am done with youth ministry because I am over twenty-five (said with sarcastic humor)? What about Deuteronomy 6?"

This goes on for a while. The challenges to their responses are not meant for discouragement, but encouragement. Encouragement to think deeply and theologically about the course of study they have chosen, to know why youth ministry matters in the church.

At the end of the semester, the question will appear again on the final. The essay question must be answered correctly, which means more than merely mirroring my response. Their answer must be able to pass the judgment and challenge of the church. If a defense cannot be made, they fail the test. It is that important. Most students pass the question with great depth and theological understanding.

TRUTH: YOUTH MINISTRY MATTERS.

WHY?

You will not find the term "youth minister" in the Bible. Instead, you will find the words "apostle," "prophet," "evangelist," "pastor," and "teacher."

> So Christ himself gave the apostles, the prophets, the evangelists, the pastors and teachers, to equip his people for works of service, so that the body of Christ may be built up until we all reach unity in the faith and in the knowledge of the Son of God and become mature, attaining to the whole measure of the fullness of Christ (Eph. 4:11–13).

You will also find examples in which these people are sent to specific people groups for ministry.

> The word of the LORD came to Jonah son of Amittai: "Go to the great city of Nineveh . . . " (Jon. 1:1–2a).

> But the Lord said to Ananias, "Go! This man [Paul] is my chosen instrument to proclaim my name to

the Gentiles and their kings and to the people of
Israel"(Acts 9:15).

While Peter was wondering about the meaning of
the vision, the men sent by Cornelius found out
where Simon's house was and stopped at the gate
(Acts 10:17).

After Paul had seen the vision, we got ready at once
to leave for Macedonia, concluding that God had
called us to preach the gospel to them (Acts 16:10).

A youth minister is a minister who has been called and sent
to serve teenagers. As a missionary to the students, the reach
of one's ministry is inclusive of everyone who impacts the students' spiritual formation.

Hear, O Israel: The LORD our God, the LORD is one.
Love the LORD your God with all your heart and
with all your soul and with all your strength. These
commandments that I give you today are to be on
your hearts. Impress them on your children. Talk
about them when you sit at home and when you
walk along the road, when you lie down and when
you get up. Tie them as symbols on your hands
and bind them on your foreheads. Write them on
the doorframes of your houses and on your gates
(Deut. 6:4–9).

The responsibility spoken of in this familiar passage is inclusive
of everyone who impacts the spiritual formation of children.
Parents, adults, and all other influencers have a responsibility
to impress the way of the Lord upon children.

HOW?

There are three general areas in which youth ministers work to fulfill their role as teenage culture missionaries. Those three are seen in this definition of youth ministry:

> Youth ministry exists to strategically assist parents and surrounding adults in bringing students to a saving relationship with Jesus Christ, to assist in equipping them for life and eternity and to assist in a student's assimilation into the life of the church.[1]

"Assist" is a key word in this definition. This word is used to remind youth ministers and leaders that ministry to students is inclusive of and makes use of the entire body of believers. In other words, whether you have a student directly involved in youth group or not, we are all youth ministers.

The three general activity areas provide a road map for how youth ministers fulfill their responsibilities.

Bring students to a saving relationship with Jesus Christ. This is the central focus of all ministers. It is the standing order of our Lord. The term "saving relationship" indicates the importance of gathering disciples (followers), not decisions (fans).[2]

Equip them for life and eternity. Disciples (followers) need instruction. Scripture is filled with teachings that equip the followers of Christ to walk in holiness and with eyes toward eternity.[3]

Assimilate them into the life of the church. Each disciple (follower) has a place, purpose, and responsibility for service in the church.[4] There is not a special body of believers exclusively designed for teenagers. Youth ministers constantly work to assist students in finding their place in the body of believers.[5]

These three guideposts also beg the questions: Why do we need a youth minister to assist our students? Is this not the responsibility of parents?

Keep in mind that youth ministers assist, rather than replace, the work of parents and other adults in a student's life. Also, remember the strategic focus of a youth minister. Like a missionary trained to work with a foreign culture, youth ministers are trained to work with and within teenage culture.

It has been my experience that youth ministers who understand themselves as ministers, culturally focused missionaries, and assistants in the spiritual formation of students rarely face a challenge as to their role in the ministry of the church.

 ## NOW?

Youth ministry matters. It is a defensible and a powerful tool in assisting the body of Christ in the spiritual formation of their students.

Defend your ministry. Prepare yourself to explain why and how you work in youth ministry. If you cannot do this, use this chapter as a starting point, and dig deeply and theologically into the validity of your ministry.

Live into your calling. You know your role and function. Everyone will not understand your ministry and say things like:

> "When are you going to grow up and become
> a preacher?"
> "How long can you keep playing with these kids?"
> "I wish I had a job that would let me take off to the
> mountains for a week!"

I have heard all of these. No need to get defensive and feel unappreciated. Keep working! The quality of your ministry will silence your critics.

Embrace your calling. Do not worry if you've never experienced a "burning bush" moment that brought you into the ministry. Many full-time youth ministers began their ministry as a volunteer or summer intern. They saw a need (or were asked to fill a spot), and fell in love with youth ministry. Perhaps you are a trusted parent or adult volunteer who answered the call for help. However you arrived, welcome to the mission field.

"You can't do this forever!"

I understand the motivation behind the pastor who spoke those words to me, and I took no offense. He was encouraging me to take another ministry position, and I was honored by his confidence. But, I told him, I am not done with youth ministry. I wanted to expand the influence and oversight of the youth ministry, and he wanted to expand my influence and oversight outside the youth ministry. It was evident that he did not totally understand youth ministry as I speak of it in this chapter. He thought of it as a young person's ministry.

To be fair, I do not "do" youth ministry the same way I did when I was nineteen. So, in that sense, I could not and no longer do "that" type of youth ministry. My tempo and style has evolved through the years. Still, today, I am much more effective and better equipped to assist parents and adults in the spiritual formation of teenagers than when I was nineteen years old.

Like many of my older youth minister friends, our cultural focus is teenagers, but our ministry is with and through the church body.

Due to creativity and mentoring of younger coworkers and volunteers, youth ministry is becoming a grown person's ministry. Why the maturing of youth ministry professionals? Because youth ministry has a defensible and theological purpose inside the church.

CONCLUDING TRUTH: YOUTH MINISTRY MATTERS.

End
Matter

Youth Ministry Programming Process

We all do it. We replicate the programming we grew up with or experienced in our internship when beginning our own youth ministry. However, this will not be effective for long. Learn how to evaluate your own context of ministry.

If you have inherited a youth ministry program, there are programs that will need to be kept and others you will want to change or get rid of entirely. There will also be "sacred cow" programs that will be close to impossible to change, and not without great effort and challenge.[1] Learning how to evaluate your context of ministry will give you the information you need to bring change to a program and even lead a "sacred cow" to slaughter.

Chap Clark taught me this formula, and it has proven to be the most effective method for developing contextual youth ministry programming that I have ever used: *Needs + Resources = Programming*. For a full explanation of this process, read his chapter in *Starting Right: Thinking Theologically about Youth Ministry*. A reductionist view of the process formula is provided below for quick startup assistance.

Needs. These include the actual and perceived needs of adolescents and their families. You can find the needs of your ministry context by working through the following questions:

* What are the general needs of all students and families?
* What are the contextual needs of the students and families in your community?
* What are the specific needs of the students and families attending your church?

These questions can be answered in groups (volunteers, leaders, parents, students) or by yourself. The more information gathered, the better.

The assimilation of the information will begin to fall into natural categories, allowing you to develop a need-based programming target. Caution: You and your team will be moved by the needs that you discover and will want to jump to the programming portion of the planning. Resist the urge. The resources piece is crucial to your programming success.

Resources. What do you have at your disposal that can be leveraged for ministry purposes? Do not overthink this—it is an inventory, not a wish list.

* How big is your budget?
* Do you have transportation?
* Do you have a youth room?
* Do you have sound equipment?
* Do you have a kitchen?
* Do you live near a park?
* Do you have motivated adult volunteers?
* Do people in your church like teenagers?
* Does your senior pastor support youth ministry?

This is not an exhaustive list of questions. Take inventory of your physical, emotional, and spiritual resources. This is important because you cannot create, execute, or follow up with any youth ministry program without needed resources.

With these two steps completed, you have a clear picture of what needs should be targeted and what you have available to develop a program to meet those needs. Programming is the fun part.

Programming. How are you going to meet the needs you have identified with the resources you have available? Again, this is the fun part in which you and your group can create and dream together. This is also the point in which existing programs should be evaluated for effectiveness. Change is difficult in the best of circumstances. However, the process you have completed gives you the needed information to change or discontinue programming that no longer meets a need and/or no longer has the resources to sustain itself.

One last word concerning change: Every program started from a desire to meet a perceived or real need. Be careful not to unduly criticize and tear apart the programming of others. Honor their work.

Is Youth Ministry for You?

After asking my Introduction to Youth Ministry students to defend the practice of youth ministry in the church,[2] this is the second question I ask them. Why? Because what drew them into the youth ministry may not be what will keep them in it for the long haul.

Most of us enjoyed our youth group experiences and saw little of the behind-the-scenes messiness and challenges our youth minister experienced. Our view of youth ministry is from the mountaintops, not the valleys. As you know, the view from below is much different than the view from the heights. Therefore, I help my students process their calling by asking them a series of strategic questions.

Start with Jim Burns' three questions. Jim is a youth ministry pioneer who left a deep impact in the direction and theology of youth ministry. He believes you are experiencing "call" when you can answer the following three questions in the affirmative:

* Do you see the need?
* Do you feel overwhelmed by the need?
* Do you have the desire to do something about that need?

In his opinion, when you are overwhelmed by the need, God does the work. When you desire to do something, you join God in that work.

Mapping and challenging your journey into youth ministry. These questions are designed to assist students in looking back at their spiritual journey and forward into the reality and challenge of youth ministry:

* Why are you here? What brought you to the point of wanting to be a youth minister?
* How much "applause" do you receive for your involvement with youth ministry?
* What will happen when the "applause" dies down or disappears? Would you still choose youth ministry? Why?
* What are the "negative" voices saying about your career choice? Do they have a point?
* What do your parents and/or guardians think of your journey into youth ministry?
* What do you know about the challenging side of youth ministry? Do you enjoy the seventy percent enough to put up with the thirty percent of challenge?
* How do you handle conflict?
* How is your relationship with:
  ○ Your family and friends?
  ○ Teenagers?
  ○ Authority figures?
  ○ Those better than you?
  ○ Your spouse or significant other?
  ○ God?

Each of these questions can result in deep introspection. However, by the end, a student has a pretty good understanding of what they are signing up for in youth ministry.

Going back to Jim's questions, I am not asking for a "burning bush" moment. I am just asking for a committed willingness to bring Jesus into the brokenness of teenage culture.

Challenging your understanding of youth ministry. This simple "what it's not" list is involved throughout the discernment process. Youth ministry is not:

* A place to find your best friends
* A place to find a spouse
* A place to find significance
* A place to find your identity
* A place to avoid adults and adult responsibilities
* A stepping stone into the pulpit or real ministry

When is it time to leave? This question falls outside the scope of this book, but it should be addressed briefly. I have three pieces of advice. One, if a crisis is pushing you out of youth ministry or to another church, wait until the crisis has passed to make your decision. Two, work through the above questions. Perhaps you are being called to another church, another type of ministry, or into the secular work world to be a light in that environment. Working backwards will help you make a decision. And three, pray this prayer: "Lord, move me or plant me!" Then listen. Don't be surprised if you have no overwhelming feeling to stay or go. Often, God gives you a choice.

Phrases That Matter

There are a number of concepts, ideas, and motivations that have been synthesized into concise phrases. Below are some of my favorites, followed by a short explanation and the reason I value them deeply. Some are original to me, and some come from those who have influenced me and continue to impact my ministry.

It all comes down to relationship and relevance. Youth ministers all have their own relationships with Jesus. The relevance of those relationships is demonstrated by the way they live their lives. The teachings of youth ministers are authenticated by the relationship they have with the information and the relevance of the application they offer. This phrase reminds me that the level of impact I wish to have in ministry is directly related to the level of impact I allow Jesus and his teachings to have on my own life.

There is only one Savior of the world; there will never be another, and you are not him. As a student and into my adult years, I placed too much pressure on my own abilities to save the world and fix everyone's problems. I was tired and on the verge of burnout when my youth minister pulled me aside and spoke these words into my heart. This phrase reminds me that my job is to be faithful with the abilities and time the Lord has given me to use for the ministry. Jesus, not David, is the answer to the world's pain.

You are not as great or bad as people say you are. You can only be you. As a student and into my adult years, I carried a lot of anxiety and weight of concern that my efforts and accomplishments never quite met expectations. Again, my youth minister spoke these words into my heart. This phrase reminds me that I cannot let criticism or praise define my ministry and cloud my identity as a child of God. Even though I am prone to judge the success of ministry against success of others, God loves me just the way I am and wants me to use my unique gifts for youth ministry.

Don't be wrong in being right. Painfully, I have learned that a wrong attitude, defensive postures, poor choices of words, and combative presentation styles can make you wrong even when your position is right. The phrase reminds me to watch my attitude, posture, word choice, and presentation style when involved in a difficult conversation.

If you have nothing better to offer, keep your opinions to yourself. I heard these words spoken by a youth ministry legend, my youth minister's youth minister, my grandfather in youth ministry, "Big" Don Williams. He was speaking to a group of young youth ministers who thought they knew it all. This phrase reminds me to be slow to criticize until I think through my complaint and have something better to suggest for moving forward.

Kids deserve a chance to prove themselves. I am saddened by the way those who work with students pass up "helpful" information to the next grade of teachers, coaches, and youth ministers.

> "This kid is great!"
> "This kid will be a problem!"
> "This kid's family will be a blessing!"
> "This kid's family will cause you trouble!"

Such information may or may not prove helpful. Sadly, I have seen students placed in identity penalty boxes that destroyed their confidence and ability to improve themselves. This phrase reminds me to get to know a student and his or her family for myself.

People over programs. There will always be interruptions in a youth minister's day. Yes, your time, planned and otherwise, should be managed appropriately. However, when faced with a decision to set aside working on an upcoming event for the sake of ministering to a person, the person wins. This phrase reminds me to focus on the reason I do what I do as a youth minister. It is the people, not the program.

What leaks leads. Jesus said, "the mouth speaks what the heart is full of" (Luke 6:45b). Certainly, this is true of our words, but also our actions. Our leadership, positive or negative, comes from that which pours out of our hearts. This phrase reminds me to keep pouring positive and true things into my heart.

Strive for diversity. Churches, if not careful, become homogeneous communities that exclude those who are "different." What is the unique witness to the world in such church communities? This phrase reminds me to authentically engage and welcome diverse groups (socioeconomic, school choice, ethnicity, gender) into the fellowship of the church.

You become what you measure. How do you determine success in your youth ministry? What do you measure? Look at what a church measures, and you will quickly know its priorities. Be careful, and think through what and how you will measure.[3] This phrase reminds me to look beyond the vertical and work toward a horizontal view in determining youth ministry effectiveness.

Live life for those who are going to be around your bed when you die. This phrase is king of them all. It provides balance to my schedule, insight for career decisions, and the ability to say "no" when ministry wants me to say "yes." The group around my bed will be small, but I want to be sure they all want to be by my side when I die. Yes, it is morbid, but this phrase reminds me of the importance of keeping my private and public life in order.

Endnotes

Acknowledgments

[1] *Band of Brothers*, episode 10, "Points," directed by Mikael Salomon, 2001, DVD.

The Bible Matters

[1] I am not concerned as to whether the Bible will withstand a challenge. I am also not advocating for a Bible-centric view of faith or for devaluing other sources of truth.

[2] Using biblical passages to prove a point you are making without regard to the actual context of the passage.

[3] Logos Bible Study Tools (www.logos.com) and Bible Gateway (www .biblegateway.com) are great online resources. The Logos tools are provided at a cost but bring wonderful, traditional print copy resources to the youth minister's immediate disposal.

Boundaries Matter

[1] A good resource to consider reading is *Boundaries* by Henry Cloud and John Townsend.

Budgets Matter

[1] For example, you may decide to lower the price of an activity so that more students can participate. In doing so, the amount of money you take in is lowered, resulting in an overspending situation. Or, more students showed up than expected and you had to feed them (this is a more defendable situation).

The Church Matters

[1] Kara E. Powell and Chap Clark, *Sticky Faith: Everyday Ideas to Build Lasting Faith in Your Kids* (Grand Rapids: Zondervan, 2011).

[2] Powell and Clark, *Sticky Faith*.

Conflict Matters

[1] "Resolution" is a loaded word. It does not imply that there are no consequences given or suffered from sinful or hurtful action. It does mean that some level of appropriate relationship has been restored. The resources given in this chapter will assist in further explaining healthy resolution.

[2] These are a few of my favorite resources on conflict management: *Helping People Forgive* by David W. Augsburger, *Controlling the Cost of Conflict* by Karl A. Slaikeu and Ralph H. Hasson, *Church Conflict* by Charles H. Cosgrove and Dennis D. Hatfield, *Meeting the Moment* by G. Douglas Lewis, *When Push Comes to Shove* by Karl A. Slaikeu, *Managing the Congregation* by Norman Shawchuck and Roger Heuser, and *Managing Church Conflict* by Hugh F. Halverstadt.

[3] This verse has nothing to do with the worship assembly. It has to do with reconciliation.

[4] To get a great understanding of systems and how they function in a church, work through *Generation to Generation: Family Process in Church and Synagogue* by Edwin H. Friedman.

[5] A withdrawal is not avoidance. Withdrawal indicates that a time-out has been called to settle emotions and that a promise has been made to resume discussion at a later date.

[6] Search "conflict style inventory" and you will find a number of assessments. Caution: As with all things Internet, there are a number of free inventories that may or may not be legitimate.

Entertainment Matters

[1] See Relationships Matter.

[2] See Safety Matters.

[3] Simply search for definitions of the words "holiness," "righteousness," or "purity" (any form of these words), and you will see the care and concern we should take when choosing an entertainment option.

Marriage Matters

[1] Actually, for the next thirteen years, my leaders would not allow Lisa and me to teach for extended periods of time without regular breaks in which we were expected to attend a class or small group not related to youth ministry.

Mission Trips and Service Projects Matter

[1] The Green Lawn Church of Christ bus accident on May 2, 1999.

Organization Matters

[1] Others may divide the youth minister's year into other "seasons," but this method has served me well through the years.

[2] Use the Youth Ministry Programming Process section in the End Matter section as a resource for planning.

[3] See Volunteers Matter.

[4] If there is not a formal coaching program available through your denominational convention, ask an older youth minister for time. There is a formal interdenominational coaching program offered by Youth Specialties. Information on the YS 101 Collaborative can be found on its website at https://youthspecialties.com/.

Outreach Matters

[1] Read *Hurt 2.0* by Chap Clark for a better understanding on what is going on inside today's adolescent culture.

[2] A strong "If you die today, will you go to heaven or hell?" type of message. To be clear, there is nothing wrong with this type of message. Just don't surprise your guests.

Physical Health Matters

[1] As with all strenuous activity, check with your doctor before starting any new workout program.

[2] There are stretches that can help lengthen your spine, hamstring, and shoulders. Ask any athletic trainer, physical therapist, or medical doctor in your church. You can also search the Internet.

Relationships Matter

[1] For more information about the Fuller Youth Institute initiative, visit www.stickyfaith.org.

[2] Origin unknown. I first heard this statement from Chap Clark.

Retreats and Camps Matter

[1] See Teaching Matters.

[2] I am a huge advocate of intergenerational ministry. An adult with the ability to hang out with, talk to, and process information with a student is your most valuable retreat resource. With that said, an adult who does not relate well with students and has no job to do can create an awkward circumstance.

Self-Care Matters

[1] On my busiest of days, I will read and meditate on one verse, or I will pick a Psalm or Proverb to reflect on to start my day.

Sexual Purity Matters

[1] Pornography should not be narrowly defined as video consumption. Literature, cartoons, print and online advertisements, social media sites, and video/computer games can all be used to access erotic or pornographic material. Especially in today's cyber society, pornography can be found on cell phones, computers, and gaming platforms. In other words, pornography is not difficult to find and access for people of any gender, of any age, or from any location.

[2] Covenant Eyes, Safe Eyes, and X3 Watch are all worth examining for accountability and safety on the Internet.

Teaching Matters

[1] Rick Atchley is a wonderful friend and mentor. He is a master craftsman of teaching and has helped me a great deal in the area of focusing the message.

Volunteers Matter

[1] Superhero youth ministers are youth ministers who do everything themselves and use volunteers sparingly or not at all. They don't wear a mask, but they might as well. No one really knows the needs of the youth minister or ministry.

[2] Christian Smith and Melinda Lundquist Denton, *Soul Searching: The Religious and Spiritual Lives of American Teenagers* (Oxford: Oxford University Press, 2005).

[3] Be sure to check with your church accountant about the monetary limit for volunteer gifts.

Worship Matters

[1] Many use Hebrews 10:24–25 as a legalistic command to assembly. Church attendance will not be counted as a condition of salvation. If this is your view, I respectfully ask you to examine this verse in its beautiful context. We assemble to encourage one another, not to check an item off a to-do list. I did not say the worship assembly is unimportant or not a reflection of our seriousness to pursue the way of Christ. Worship is critical to a believer's growth.

[2] If the word "acceptable" gets you sidetracked on mode and style, read the verse in context. Acceptable worship has much more to do with focus, personal holiness, and relationships. Again, context is key.

[3] Research the actual need for and function of disfellowshipping. If you have never seen this word, get to work and study the concept.

Youth Ministry Matters

[1] This definition draws from the influence of Mike Yaconelli, Chap Clark, Kara Powell, and my study on intergenerational ministry programming.

[2] The idea of being a follower, not a fan, was made popular by Kyle Idleman in *Not a Fan: Becoming a Completely Committed Follower of Jesus.*

[3] The Sermon on the Mount, Romans 12, and Ephesians 4–5 are great examples of this type of teaching.

[4] 1 Corinthians 12:12ff.

[5] That does not mean students should not be given space to explore Jesus and equip themselves for life and eternity with their peers. It does mean that constant segregation is not conducive to assimilation and is destructive to a student's spiritual formation.

End Matter

[1] "Sacred cow" programs are those that have a strong following. They have deep history with the group and are difficult to change without cost. Sometimes, messing with "sacred cow" programming can cost you your job. Be wise!

[2] For a defense and definition of youth ministry, see Youth Ministry Matters.

[3] A word about quantifying success in youth ministry: Yes, the number of students attending activities is a marker of "success," but numbers alone are not a sufficient indication of a ministry's value. And yes, it is a good thing if students, parents, and church leaders like the youth minister. But being likable is not a reliable indicator either. May I suggest we change the direction of what we count? The typical counting measure in ministry is "vertical" (e.g., we had fifty last Wednesday and sixty-five this Wednesday—the numbers are going up). But how many of those students are coming back week after week? A more accurate picture of ministry participation is done with a horizontal count (e.g., we had fifty last Wednesday and sixty-five this Wednesday—however, horizontally counting, forty-five of those students came each Wednesday, thirty-five of those also attended Sunday morning worship, and twenty-six of those students also attended the Sunday night programming). You have twenty-six students who participated in everything. The numbers are going across.

"Youthworkers who don't pay attention to families are like farmers who don't pay attention to the soil. *Owning Faith* is a welcome tool for those wise youthworkers who realize that nurturing and enriching the soil of families is one of the surest ways to impact the fruit of real life youth ministry."

—DUFFY ROBBINS,
Professor of Youth Ministry, Eastern University

OWNING FAITH

edited by **Dudley Chancey and Ron Bruner**

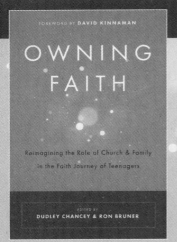

Owning Faith
$15.99

Today's adolescents face an uphill climb as they seek to own their faith. *Owning Faith* is an accessible guide into the adventure-filled, spiritual journey of adolescents. If you would like to learn how to be a wise and compassionate companion who can make an eternal difference in the lives of youth, *Owning Faith* will show you how.

LEAFWOOD
PUBLISHERS
an imprint of Abilene Christian University Press

www.leafwoodpublishers.com | 877-816-4455 (toll free)